Nationality, Birthrights and Jurisprudence
New Social & Cultural Blueprint for Melaninated Indigenous People

Written and Compiled by
Bandele El Amin

I dedicate this book to all brothers and sisters who are seekers of knowledge. To seek knowledge and wisdom despite the opinions of the 85%'ers is a test to your love and dedication. I honor you all and hope we all continue to grow with knowledge and wisdom.

For more information about special discounts for bulk [wholesale] please contact Bandele El Amin at 937-422-3431 or indigenouspeoplesnetwork@hotmail.com. Check out the website at indigenousservices.webs.com

The information in this book is a compilation of information from various sources and original writing. Any legal information is for educational purposes only.

CONTENTS

INTRODUCTION

The purpose of this manual is to give Moors a better grasp of law and history. The rise of the Moorish consciousness is blooming as we head into the new Age of Aquarius. There's resistance by the courts to recognize our Moorish heritage. They must be made to understand the power of the Free National Moors, who inhabit the Northwest and Southwest shores of Amexem[1]. Our mission is to uplift fallen humanity. *"The Prophet Noble Drew Ali said that money doesn't make a man, it's Free National power and standards that make a man."*

---

[1] Amexem is the name of Africa and the Americas prior to separation millions of years ago used my Moorish Americans.

CHAPTER ONE
LET US BEGIN

The purpose of this project was to teach Africans in America about Moorish/African centered culture, history, nationality and how to apply it to the laws of their community. The manual will create a blueprint for future generations to regain lost knowledge and first class Citizenship.

Black communities have existed in Colonial cities since the late 1700s. The community of today faces many challenges similar to that of recent ancestors. Lack of resources and power over communities has become more a problem than before. The African American Negro has faced segregation, slavery, discrimination, lynching, hangings and Jim Crow. Today, Black students see lower performance on test scores, lack of Black ownership, police harassment and limited food/retail sources. Crime and incarceration rank high among social issues affecting the Black community. Drug related crime is extremely higher among Blacks. Ninety percent of federal crack cocaine defendants are Black.[2] Increased drug sales correlate with poverty. A quote from well-known Pan African scholar Dr. Amos Wilson says:

---

[2] Pg. 142 in *No Equal Justice* by David Cole

"Increases in homelessness, poverty, unemployment, criminality and violence in the Black community; disorganization of the traditional Black family, inadequacies in education, increases in health problems of all types, and a host of other social and political ills have all attended increases in the number of Black elected and appointed officials. That is, the more elected and appointed Black politicians, the more social-economic problems the Black community has suffered."3

In Trotwood, Ohio, Black communities have diverse incomes however the results are the same. Trotwood has a large Black community. As a resident of Trotwood for over 20 years, there had been a continual shift in ethnicity from white to Black. A perfect example is Black white ratios in my schools from 1979 to 1991. In 1979, there were 20:4 ratios of whites to Blacks. In 1991, the numbers had reversed to 18:5 ratio favoring Blacks to whites. The exodus of the whites caused a decline in business investments with few options. What is the future for the former slaves? Why are Blacks at the bottom of the economical, sociological and political ladders? Crime and poverty are parallel in a society where the value of

---

3 Blueprint for Black Power: A Moral, Political, and Economic Imperative for the Twenty-First Century"--pages 27-29]

currency falls yearly. Street crimes are higher among Blacks. Property value drops in the Black community and paying higher mortgage rates. Eating selections in Black communities are low. The majority of restaurants, in urban communities are fast food i.e. Taco Bell, McDonalds, Burger King and KFC. The educated are not respected or acknowledged with equality. The educated Black elite like Michael Eric Dyson or Cornell West play second to Dr. Phil or Dr. Oz.

Heavy amounts of Black community financial support come from the state and federal. Government grants (501 c3s) usage by many Black churches and private schools (charter schools) increase yearly. The majority of Black communities' spend money outside their own neighborhoods. Primary reason Black's spend money outside their community is because majority of optimal resources are found in other communities. The money spent within their own community in many cases go to a foreigner from another nation and community. Many organizations that are in place to assist Blacks are outdated and declining in influence. The N.A.A.C.P. SNCC, and Rainbow coalition are just a couple. The key to uplifting the Black community does not come from organizations using "played out" tactics. The Black communities must adapt to the new paradigm.

Slavery plays a crucial key in the puzzle of the Blacks psyche. The story of a man called *Willie Lynch* give a clear description of the atrocities witnessed by Black slaves against themselves, fellow comrades and family members. Here is an excerpt from the Willie Lynch letter:

> *"I caught the whiff of a dead slave hanging from a tree a couple of miles back. You are not only losing valuable stock by hangings, you are having uprisings, slaves are running away, your crops are sometimes left in the fields too long for maximum profit, you suffer occasional fires, your animals are killed, gentlemen...you know what your problems are; I do not need to elaborate. I am not here to enumerate your problems; I am here to introduce you to a method of solving them. In my bag here, I have a foolproof method for controlling your Black slaves. I guarantee every one of you that if installed correctly it will control the slaves for at least 300 years. My method is simple, any member of your family or any overseer can use it"*[4]

From reading that phrase, you must quickly gather that slaves were a big issue and the need for control was an even bigger. Using brainwashing techniques, the slave

---

[4] Pg. 1 of Willie Lynch Letter

master would subdue the Black slaves similar to that of, "breaking a horse". The theory is that you break a "nigger" like you tame a wild horse. Directly through slavery, Africans in America were dehumanized and placed in second-class citizenship. Slavery created a holocaust that murdered many Blacks and changed a people forever. The horrific depictions of slavery haunt the psyche of Black's every day. The African race was stripped of its culture and nationality which is the 3/5 clause located in the constitution.[5] Small remnants of culture found in song, art and Black churches. I believe that slavery, Jim Crow and outright racism played a major part in why Blacks are introverted. Another part of the problem stems from loss of connection to any ancient national creed and culture. Without a nationality, Blacks are detached from the human family. Nationality connects people to culture, history and self pride. Everyone who came to the United States had a nationality. The Black, African slaves are the only group of people not to have their nationality. Similar to an adopted child, who has no history of their biological parents, the Black race has no history or national ties to ancient ancestors. The child doesn't know the family history. Any journey in life is more pleasant when you are not confused and lost. Lost is the best way to describe the African Black slaves of the diaspora. Lost in the

---

[5] Article 1 section 3 of the U.S. Constitution

present because the loss of the past; now the future is unclear.

The problem Blacks' face in the 21st century find their origin thousands of years ago with the defeat of Egypt (KMT) in 325 BCE by Alexander the Greek. Egypt, which originally called Kemet (Ta Meri), was the center of culture for the Ancient world. Located in North Afrika, Egypt gave the world science, philosophy, medicine, mathematics and religion. The significance of Egypt is that it was African in origin. According to Dr. Cheikh Anta Diop, many Pharaohs were Black or Africanoid in origin. These concepts are laid out in Diop's *"TOWARDS THE AFRICAN RENAISSANCE: ESSAYS IN CULTURE AND DEVELOPMENT, 1946-1960,; "The Cultural Unity of Black Africa: The Domains of Patriarchy and of Matriarchy in Classical Antiquity,* These concepts can be summarized as follows:

Southern Cradle-Egyptian Model:

1. Abundance of vital resources.

2. Sedentary-agricultural.

3. Gentle, idealistic, peaceful nature with a spirit of justice.

4. Matriarchal family.

5. Emancipation of women in domestic life.

6. Territorial state.

7. Xenophilia.

8. Cosmopolitanism.

9. Social collectivism.

10. Material solidarity - alleviating moral or material misery

11. Idea of peace, justice, goodness and optimism.

12. Literature emphasizes novel tales, fables and comedy.

Northern Cradle-Greek Model:

1. Bareness of resources.

2. Nomadic-hunting (piracy)

3. Ferocious, warlike nature with spirit of survival.

4. Patriarchal family.

5. Debasement/enslavement of women.

6. City state (fort)

7. Xenophobia.

8. Parochialism.

9. Individualism.

10. Moral solitude.

11. Disgust for existence, pessimism.

12. Literature favors tragedy.

This assessment by Diop demonstrates the stability and cultural identity of Black Egyptians. These Black Egyptians practiced a peaceful lifestyle and enjoyed prosperity. It was the warlike attitude of the Greeks that created the first ripple in the decline of Black African dominance in the world. The Greeks would learn the sciences of Egypt and build the foundations of western civilization upon them. Rome saw rise and conflict with Africa as inevitable. Hannibal of Carthage against Rome fought the Punic wars, in 264 BCE. Rome won the war and the people of Carthage were sold into slavery and crucified across the countryside. After the fall of Rome in the 6th and 7th centuries, Europe goes into a great depression known as the "Dark Ages." During this time, the African known as the Moors began to take dominance in the world. These Black Moors, known for controlling Spain (Iberian Peninsula) for 700 years. These Moors built the only College in Europe (Cordova). The Moors are to be very influential in the history of the Black slaves in America. They are the vital key in African American culture. The 1491 defeat of the Moors in Spain was the turning point for Blacks and the beginning of chattel slavery and New World Order. The Moors were the last Black stronghold against the Europeans whom began to climb out the Dark Ages emerging in the Renaissance age. The age of enlightenment and humanist thought brought the European into the age of exploration. Christopher Columbus starts the age of exploration and

European discovery of America would prove disastrous to the African Moors in the old and new world.

Slavery was not exclusive to Europeans during conquest of the New World. The Arab slave trade was the practice of slavery in the Arab world, mainly in Western Asia, North Africa, Southeast Africa, the Horn of Africa and certain parts of Europe (such as Iberia and Sicily) during the era of the Arab conquests. The trade was focused on the slave markets of the Middle East, North Africa and the Horn of Africa. People traded were not limited to a certain race, ethnicity, or religion.

During the 8th and 9th centuries of the Fatimid Caliphate[6], most of the slaves were Europeans (called Saqaliba) captured along European coasts and during wars. Historians estimate that between 650 and 1900, to 18 million peoples were enslaved by Arab slave traders and taken from Europe, Asia and Africa across the Red Sea, Indian Ocean, and Sahara desert. However, slaves were drawn from a wide variety of regions and included Mediterranean peoples, Persians, peoples from the Caucasus mountain regions (such

6 The **Fatimid Islamic Caliphate** or **al-Fātimiyyūn** (Arabic na saw (ال فاطم يون)
Arabo-Berber Shia Muslim caliphate first centered in Tunisia and later in
Egypt that ruled over varying areas of the Maghreb, Sudan, Sicily, Malta, the
Levant, and Hijaz from 5 January 909 to 1171.

as Georgia, Armenia and Circassia) and parts of Central Asia and Scandinavia, English,Dutch and Irish, Berbers from North Africa, and various other peoples of varied origins as well as those of African origins.

Toward the 18th and 19th centuries, the flow of Zanj (Bantu) slaves from Southeast Africa increased with the rise of the Oman sultanate, which was based in Zanzibar in Tanzania. They came into direct trade conflict and competition with Portuguese and other Europeans along the Swahili coast. The North African Barbary states carried on piracy against European shipping and enslaved thousands of European Christians. They earned revenues from the ransoms charged; in many cases in Britain, village churches and communities would raise money for such ransoms. The British government did not ransom its citizens.

Understanding of Moorish history connects Blacks in America today. The Moorish connection is essential for Blacks in America to regain their Nationality and citizenship lost during slavery. Slavery is the very cause of the problem because it dehumanized a continent of people. Slavery denationalized millions of Africans and classified them under one generic status. Gradual decline of Afro-centric influence and eventual sever of cultural identity was the aftermath of losing to European Nations.

The slave titles like Black, colored, African American, Afro American, nigger and Negro are titles for a nation less people.

The Moorish Science Republic of New Kemit is a civic government designed to uplift fallen humanity. It derives it fundamental design from the original members of the Moorish Science Temple of America 1928. The MSR of NK is a self-governing society developed and inspired from the Egyptian principle Maat[7]/Maa. This "society" is to practice and teach African centered philosophy, thought and ritual. The idea of this government is to educate Blacks of their Moorish/African heritage, restore their Moorish nationality and collect reparations for slavery and Jim Crow. MSR of NK serves the people to understand law and how to retain their human (sovereign/constitutional) rights through nationality. Nationality will create unification of the Black population through a common agenda. To create a political movement that has the power to create change. The scope of this project is grand however, it will look at the primary steps required to create a paradigm shift in Black

---

7 **Maat** or **ma'at** (thought to have been pronounced *[muʔ.ʕat]), also spelled **māt** or **mayet**, was the ancient Egyptian concept of truth, balance, order, **law**, morality, and justice. Maat was also personified as a goddess regulating the stars, seasons, and the actions of both mortals and the deities, who set the order of the universe from chaos at the moment of creation. Her (ideological) counterpart wasIsfet.

consciousness of African Diaspora. The Constitution of the United States calls it to be done. The Constitution of the United States calls for every man to proclaim his own nationality and religion, and then you are a true citizen of the United States. Look at the difference from being a citizen and a true Citizen. Through the Moorish paradigm, the Black problem can be solved. Nationality pertains to the fallen sons and daughters of Moorish descent. Nationality the only channel through which the former slave and their children may become true citizens of this Free National Republic of the United States and this is according to the law and constitution of this Government.

Nationality can be found in religious text. Making a comparison with the Leviticus Code, only through an established Government representing the Nation in which Blacks have descendant that you can receive your true citizenship papers, your recognition, your rights and your true sense of freedom as a Moorish American in these Shores. The Book of Leviticus in the Bible is a seminal document, in many ways more profound than the United States Declaration of Independence or Constitution. How? Leviticus sets in order the priesthood, and by default, organized religion. Secondly, it contains the form of a universal code of civil law that now rules not only Israel, but also most of Western civilization. Although

Hammurabi's Code[8] *(Babylon) predates "Moses' Law,"* *the Leviticus code can be seen far more predominantly in governments everywhere. Leviticus 8:5 - "And Moses said unto the congregation, this is the thing which the LORD commanded to be done." So regardless of how many tribal names in Africa, they are all universally Moors and the Noble Drew Ali told us that there were tribes of the Moors (El, Bey & Ali). The Tribal names of El or Bey connect back to Moorish descent through the connection of MSR of NK that will be recognized by this government, for the MSR of NK is Common Law incorporated within this Government. Therefore, either Black person is a Moorish American or a certified Negro from the city and state that they live in. Either you are a Moorish American under the Constitution or the property of the State residing. The Free National Name is Moorish American and the tribal names of El and Bey links Blacks across the Diaspora to the culture and beliefs of the forefathers, the vine and fig tree. The Sundry Free Moors who petitioned The House of Representatives were deemed subjects of Morocco and we are the descendants of the Sundry Free Moors. Taking tribal titles of El ,Bey, Ali, Muhammad, Al or Dey in addition to proclaiming Moorish Citizenship of the MSR of NK or any other establish Moorish body and the Moorish National Movement. MSR of NK is*

---

8 The Code of Hammurabi is a well-preserved Babylonian law code of ancient Iraq, formerly Mesopotamia, dating back to about 1772 BC. It is one of the oldest deciphered writings of significant length in the world.

descendents of Moroccans(Moors) (North Western & South Western Afrika) and born in America, making us Moorish Americans, becoming paramount and qualified. A member in a political government under the MSR of NK creates dual citizenship because both America and the MSR of NK are body politics placing Moors under article 4 section 2 of the U.S. Constitution (2.1 Clause 1: Privileges and Immunities) and through our descent nature that the Moroccan-American Friendship Treaty and agreements recognize Moors. It was through the 14th Amendment of the U.S. Constitution, that African Americans after 1865 were certified as American born Negroes, Blacks and colored people, which derives from the word nature. As original people of the Americas, we are also protected by Louisiana Purchase Treaty of April 30, 1803-Article 3[9]. The Washitaw nation is proof that treaty. The terms Negro, Black, and colored are unnatural and are contrary to our fundamental nature. Honorable Marcus Garvey stated, "The flag of a Nation is the emblem that signifies the existence of that Nation."

---

[9] **Article III**

The inhabitants of the ceded territory shall be incorporated in the Union of the United States and admitted as soon as possible according to the principles of the federal Constitution to the enjoyment of all these rights, advantages and immunities of citizens of the United States, and in the mean time they shall be maintained and protected in the free enjoyment of their liberty, property and the Religion which they profess.

The MSR of NK flag, the red, black and green flag with the green five-pointed star in the center represents the Divine Creed, Principles and existence of the Moorish Nation. The Ancient Moorish Flag was restored to the Moors in the year 1925 by Noble Drew Ali. Noble Drew Ali brought the red flag with the green star in the center. This testifies to the fact that a melanin Nation existed prior to our enslavement. We are the descendants of the Ancient Moabites, the aboriginal inhabitants of North, South and Central America (originally named Amexem). A man gets his nationality from the geographical landmass that his ancestors inhabited. So we are descendants of African (the Free Sundry Moors) and born in America. The beginning of the making of Negroes occurred September 5th 1774 in the state of Pennsylvania in the city of Philadelphia (the first capital of the United States of America). The government classifies the Negro (Colored, Blacks, Afro Americans, African Americans) as being stateless. A Moorish American must be conscious and conscientious of his or her nationality, Birthright, Constitutional Heritage, and upholding the Divine Creed and Principles of their Ancient Forefathers. This means the Negro has no citizenship in America, which is where he or she was born. A Negro has no country of his own. The Negro's citizenship in the countries of Africa stripped from them. The Negro does not truly have an American Nationality. The Negro is a person born without being a citizen of any country. Africa does not renounce the

Negro, but the Negro cannot be recognized by Africa, because the right of blood relationship to Africa has been stripped away from the Negro. So the Negro cannot say what his Nationality is, and even though the Negro is born in America, it does not see the Negro as an American citizen. In America, the Negro is a person whom is not a citizen of any country and his rights in America are lower than that of an illegal alien. A Negro's legal position is much worse than that of an illegal alien, because a Negro has no government to which a Negro can appeal for protection outside of the U.S. Negroes are a displaced (do not have the right of blood relationship to any country) and stateless (do not have citizenship in any country) people. In this country, the Negro has little or no civic and political rights. As a Moorish American, you have true citizenship within the United States. A Moorish American's place of birth is in America (Jus Soli), but their ancestors' citizenship was Moroccan (Jus Sanguinis). As a member of a Moorish body, you become incorporated within this government of the United States of America, you have your nationalization as Moorish American. By naturalization through the Moorish Republic of New Kemit, you are Moorish American. As a Moorish American no longer fall under the 14th Amendment of the U.S. Constitution, the Black Codes or the Negro Act. As a Moorish American you are not a Negro, or 3/5 of a human. Learn the creed about your nationality and birthrights, because you are not a Negro.

You must claim a free national name to be an American citizen.

The Immigration Laws of the U.S. Constitution, states that if a person seeks citizenship they must proclaim a Free National Name before the Constitutional Government of the United States of America. (U.S. Constitution Article I, Section 8 -Congressional Authority to Establish Uniform Rules of Naturalization), (Federal Statutes 18 U.S.C., Part I, chapter 69, Review the Unites States code as it applies to Nationality and Citizenship in the context of crimes. Chapter 18 of the U.S. code. 8 U.S.C. 13, Review Chapter 13 of the United States' code establishing the Immigration and Naturalization Service). 8 U.S.C. Chapter 12 ,Review the United States Code - Chapter 12 regarding Immigration and Nationality. 8 U.S.C., Part I, chapter 69 - Nationality and Citizenship (in the context of crimes).

*The United Nation's Universal Declaration of Human Rights of Dec. 10, 1948 (Article 15, Section 1 and 2), states that everyone has the right to a Nationality. **No one shall be arbitrarily deprived of his nationality nor denied the right to change his nationality.***

CHAPTER TWO
NATION SOVEREIGNTY

Native American's Sovereignty: This text presented as the inaugural lecture in the American Indian Civics Project at Humboldt State University (Arcata, CA, USA), on October 24, 1997, sponsored by the HSU Center for Indian Community Development.

Native Americans have nationalized themselves in the form of sovereign tribes. To understand the scope of MSR OF NK. it can be compared to the Roman Catholic Church in regard to sovereign bodies.

The Catholic Church/Vatican City is a sovereign city-state created from the Lateran Treaty in 1929. The city lies inside Rome however, the boundaries are never disputed. Because Vatican City is sovereign, which means the church answers virtually to no one but the Pope?

The government of Vatican City has a unique structure. The Pope is the sovereign of the state. Legislative authority is vested in the Pontifical Commission for Vatican City State, a body of cardinals appointed by the Pope for five-year periods. Executive power is in the hands of the President of that commission, assisted by the General Secretary and Deputy General

Secretary. The state's foreign relations are entrusted to the Holy See's Secretariat of State and diplomatic service. Nevertheless, the pope has full and absolute executive, legislative and judicial power over Vatican City. He is the last absolute monarch in Europe[10].

Moorish Science Temple of America

Black Nationalism is a subject very similar to the ideology of the Moorish movement. Literature on this subject included three main eras in Black Nationalism. Immigration, Marcus Garvey Movement and Malcolm X's movement.

The early movement of Black Nationalism dealt with emigration. Many Blacks wanted to go to Africa or Latin America.

The roots of Black Nationalism in the 1800s can be found in the colonization movement, which addressed Black emigration from the United States to Africa and Latin America. McCartney suggests that a Black's desire for emigration was

---

[10] The World Fact book. Retrieved on 2007-02-22 (Wikipedia)

to gain political freedom and independence not possible for Blacks as a minority group.[11]

According to the article *Black Nationalism and the Call for Black Power,* early Black Nationalist was against abolitionist and integrationist movements. Many Blacks for nationalism disagreed with Fredrick Douglass. Martin Delaney[12] must be mentioned as a pioneer in the 1800s.

The next movement finds new life in the early 1900s. Marcus Garvey starts the Universal Negro Improvement Association (U.N.I.A.) in 1918. The U.N.I.A. created an alternative from mainstream, interracial organizations like the N.A.A.C.P. Marcus Garvey would continue with various innovative programs.

Garvey clearly used education in the form of programs and newspapers to teach Black people about economic and social uplift through collective action. Garvey's socio-political philosophy of Black Nationalism, expressed in

---

[11] (McCartney, 1992: 16)." Black Nationalism and the Call for Black Power Andrew P. Smallwood, Assistant Professor, Black Studies Department, University of Nebraska, Omaha pg. 1

[12] **Martin Robison Delany** (May 6, 1812 – January 24, 1885) was an African-American abolitionist, journalist, physician, and writer, arguably the first proponent of black nationalism; **Martin Delany** is considered to be the grandfather of Black nationalism.

the UNIA, emphasized cultural pride, social separation and economic empowerment.13

Garvey believed that Black people must believe in themselves and in their race through various educational programs: The Universal Black Cross Nurses Corps, The African Legions of the UNIA-ACL, the Universal African Motor Corps, Black Star Ship Line, Universal Factories Corporation. Garvey's mistake was trust. His long time friend was working with the F.B.I. setting him up.

Malcolm X's legacy picks up the pieces left by the Garvey movement. Malcolm's ideology is linked with the Nation of Islam. The fact Malcolm's father and Elijah Muhammed were members of the U.N.I.A. add to the legacy of Marcus Garvey and the Black Nationalist movement. Malcolm, like Marcus Garvey saw the plight of Blacks as political and global. Malcolm's departure from the Nation of Islam created the backdrop for further evolution is his thinking. Malcolm's forms the Organization of Afro-American Unity (OAAU) in 1964. The O.A.A.U. was the platform which Malcolm X would begin verbally the need for Black Nationalism. Malcolm was forming the forum to take the U.S. government

13 (Colin, 1996: 56). Black Nationalism and the Call for Black Power Andrew P. Smallwood, Assistant Professor, Black Studies Department, University of Nebraska, Omaha pg. 2

before the U.N. court charging the U.S. for slavery and other horrendous acts. Malcolm's was unsuccessful due to the assassination of his person on February 21, 1965.

Similarities in the Black Nationalist movement can be found in the Moorish Science Republic of New Kemit. The underlying theme is Black empowerment. The Black Nationalist movement is trying to mobilize the majority of Blacks with the same background to become active in making a change socially, politically and economically. Shortcomings in any movement are possible and evident in each movement discussed. The issues of infiltration by government agents i.e. F.B.I., N.S.A. or B.A.T.F. are real and seen with Elijah Muhammed, Marcus Garvey and Malcolm X. The media also played an active role in the perceptions of reality. If the media is trying to discredit you, they usually can. An excellent example is Farrakhan Muhammed. Anytime he is in the public media, he is portrayed as racist. In many instances, Farrakhan is saying what many are afraid to say. The media played a part in Malcolm and Elijah's split. In any case, it is fact that infiltration happened from U.N.I.A., Black Panther party and others (COINTELPRO).

Moorish Nationality deals with spirituality but is not to be mistaken for religion. The movement is primarily political, cultural and historical. A case that shows the strong link that developed in Europe between the words

"Black" and "Moor" is that of non-Muslim Moors. Hosts of non-Muslim figures are also described as Black and Moorish. These included the Black St. Maurice whose name translates as "like a Moor." St. Maurice, the Knight of the Holy Lance, is regarded as the greatest patron saint of the Holy Roman Empire. Rumored to be a Roman commander of Egyptian descent, Maurice is said to have gained sainthood after refusing to have his legion massacre a Christian uprising. Worshipped as early as 460AD, St. Maurice has numerous artworks and structures, even a castle, dedicated to him. The existence of three hundred images of the Black St. Maurice has been catalogued, and even today, his worship is seen within numerous cathedrals in eastern Germany. Other non-Muslim Moors include the semi-legendary Sir Morien, known as "the Black Knight" of King Arthur fame and Sir Pallamedes. The importance to teach Blacks that Moors and Muslims are not considered the same is fundamental to unity. Moorish culture is separate from and older than Islam from Arabia.

CHAPTER THREE
DESCRIPTION OF INTERVENTION

Slavery and Jim Crow have created many problems in Black peoples' lives for decades. Lack of income, education and citizenship has made Blacks victims of society ills and injustice. Much of society wants to put the problem of slavery behind them as outdated" however, the repercussions of this holocaust are a continuing ripple of effect in popular culture. Stereotypes of Black images are constantly bombarding the airwaves and other media outlets. The Black community is primarily controlled by other ethnic groups i.e. whites/Europeans, Asians, and Arabs. Blacks have been used by government agencies to distribute drugs and capitalized of the profit.

Present Black leaders hold very little power or prestige in the U.S. alternatively, in the Black community. Jesse Jackson and Al Sharpton have little impact on policies. They do not have the same platform as Marcus Garvey or Malcolm X. The fact that our leaders are looking at the problem from the same paradigm of the "Civil Rights" era is not effective. Who will stand up for their rights as human? When will our leaders teach us to be human? The objectives of MSR OF NK are to Nationalize and Educate people of their culture. I will look at these two objectives in depth.

President Barack Obama is known as the "first" Black president of the United States. The election of a Black president created a false perception of "racial" equality. Obama is not a Black leader because he governs and protects the "establishment" and its values. President Obama is a role model to young Black males however; it shifts importance of Black leadership and creates a multicultural ideology.

Objective One: Citizenship

The objective is to create a basis for Blacks to change their status in U.S. law. The ratio of Blacks going to jail or being convicted of crime can decrease severely due to the change of status a Black person claims. Change in nationality is primary focus among prisoner and law-abiding citizens. Changing nationality requires learning law (national and international) Change will happen quickly as more Blacks give up their slave titles of Black and African American. The objective is to have many prisoners that are non-violent, be released from prison due to lack of jurisdiction or defect in convictions. Learn Constitutional rights to represent in *Propia Persona*.

Description of the Intervention:

Citizenship is intervention because Blacks are not properly educated on the true nature of the U.S. law and their true status. The M.S.R.N.K. has implemented nationality classes so that Blacks would receive proper education on law. Anyone interested can enter Nationality 101. The class consists of the History of Moors in the world and in pre-Columbus America, differences between Black and Moor legally, legal definitions and terms, analyzing the U.S. Constitution, Treaty of Peace and Friendship, and applications to the present Moors. Preparation gives understanding of Affidavits filed on behalf of the citizen to properly proclaim their Nationality. Classes are held every other Monday from 7pm until 8:30pm at a disclosed location.

The **second objective** is restoring Blacks to the human race with a re-education process. This process consists of culture (history, religion, language and politics), which are missing keys in Black's psyche. Culture provides Black's with a wider viewpoint of the world to see their connection with their African National brother/sisters all across the continent. Culture shows diversity among Black people in America. African and European culture's have different perspective on the world see page 4. Many Blacks have grown accustomed to the customs of their former slave master's. To distinguish the two is absurd however, the underlining truth is that Blacks can never be so called white or have a culture of their own. Culture is what makes nations unique. Black culture is of the ancient Egyptians, Moors, Berbers, Ethiopians and practice Vodun / Animist as white culture is of Greece,

Rome, Anglo-Saxons and Catholicism/Christianity. Experts and philosophers set study classes in place to present lectures. Lecturers as: Hakim Bey, Phil Valentine, Dr. Jewel Pookrum, John Henrik Clarke, Taj Tarik Bey, Myra El, Dr, Sebi, Dr. Ivan Van Sertima and Dr. Ray Hagins teach an aspect of Afrika/Moorish culture. Study group session class are broken down into two types: (History/Nationality and Spirituality/health). Moorish Science Temple of America, founded by Noble Drew Ali, and the influence of other Islam based organizations have reformed many prisoners and helped them get early release. Moorish Science teaches knowledge that creates positive influences in their surrounding environment.

History and nationality teaches Blacks their old Sovereign titles and trace it through history. Class teaches Blacks to look at the history of Moors in the world with racial identity. Language is essential to culture. MSR of NK official language is Ki-Swahili. Ki-Swahili is widely use in Africa and many Afro centric communities in America. Class will give basics in Ki-Swahili.

The Moorish Nation here in America connect directly back to Morocco, Algiers, Tunis and Tripoli. Morocco is the very first kingdom to recognize America as a nation, the oldest and longest standing peace treaty with America is the Moroccan-American Peace Treaty of 1787. This

Treaty is very powerful because according to the U.S. Constitution, treaties are the law of the land and the U.S. Constitution is the Supreme Law of this land. The Moroccan-American Peace Treaty calls for the just and humane treatment of the Moors here in America and the only way that Blacks (the Moors) can be treated as such, is if Blacks proclaim our Nationality (Free National Name) which is Moorish American. Teaching the Moorish political influence, in West Afrika shows the connection between slaves and Moors. Many of the slaves brought to America were from the West Coast (Ivory Coast)[14] Participant groups will become familiar with Noble Drew Ali, founder of Moorish Science Temple in 1926. Noble Drew Ali's teachings will also be discussed. According to Black's Law Dictionary - 5th Editions, *"Nationality determines the political status of the individual, especially with reference to allegiance. Nationality derives from the noun Nation."*

Health and Spirituality expresses concerns of Black health. Health class gives explanations to illnesses and conditions common in Black communities i.e. high blood pressure, diabetes, A.I.D.S. and obesity. Health class will trace the history of Black diet from Afrika to slavery in America. The theme to health class is *"When you were*

---

[14] Transformation in Slavery by Paul E. Lovejoy, Cambridge University Press 2000.

brought to America, did they bring your food with you?" Health class will instruct the subjects on a vegetarian diet and its benefits. **MSR of NK** provides a history on African diet, understanding of nutrients (vitamins, minerals and herbs), melanin (skin pigmentation) and its uses, harmful chemicals in foods and natural remedies for diseases and other health conditions. Lectures from African holistic health practitioners i.e. Llalia Afrika, Dr. Sebi and Doktah B. The majority of information derives from a book entitled *"Kemetic Diet: Ancient African Wisdom for Health of Mind, Body and Spirit"* by Dr. Muata Ashby.

Spirituality deals with philosophical cultural views of Black religion. Deep study and comparison to scriptures i.e. Bible, Quran and Torah will be discussed in comparison against unfamiliar text (Book of Life and Circle 7 Koran). Spiritual class gives deeper understanding of religions text and bridge a gap between different religious groups in Black communities.

Materials needed include three-binder notebook, note pad, Black laws dictionary, and the books entitled *Wake Up Afrika, Moors, Moabite and Man* and *Muurish Treaties* written by B. El Amin.

CHAPTER FOUR
MOORISH NAMES AND THEIR MEANINGS

All people of a particular ethnic group, nationality or family have names that distinguish from others. An example of this is Jennifer Lopez. If her first name was only mentioned, you may think she was European, Albion (white) American or English. When you add her surname Lopez, the perception quickly changes to Latino. The last name of a person tells a lot about their cultural and ethnic backgrounds. Due to the enslavement of melaninated people, names and ethnic ties were cut and they were given last names of slave owners. Taking a Moorish surname ties you a family of people. It's required for all Moors to take a Moorish surname. Moorish names are Ali, Al, Bey, Dey and El. Here are brief descriptions of those names.

Bey (originally **Beg**; Arabic: كب/ *Bek*; Ottoman and Persia n: بگ / *Beg* or *Beyg*) is a Turkish title for chieftain, traditionally applied to the leaders of small tribal groups. The regions or provinces where "beys" ruled or which they administered were called *beylik*, roughly meaning "emirate" or "principality" in the first case, "province" or "governorate" in the second (the equivalent of duchy in Europe). Today, the word is still used informally as a social title for men (somewhat like the English word "mister"). Unlike "mister" however, it follows the name and is used generally with first names and not with last names. However, Moors use this as last names.

"Many elements of non-Turkic origin also became a part of Turk statecraft. Important terms, for example, often came from non-Turkic languages, as in the cases of *khatun* for the ruler's wife and *beg* for "aristocrat," both terms of Sogdian origin and ever since in common use in Turkish."

As was mentioned at the start of our discussion, and can be seen from the Wikipedia comment, *beg* is commonly known as the title *Bey*. What is interesting, and can be seen from the quote above, is that the title "Bey" is not of Turkish origin, but of Sogdian[15] origin. This word is derived from the Sogdian term *baga,* which means god. H.S. Nyberg brings this point to light in the work *Monumentum*:

"Thus it was on the basis of written evidence that the majority of the native *Sogdian* divinities were assumed to

---

15 **Sogdiana** (/ˌsɔːgdiˈænə/ or /ˌsɒgdiˈænə/)
or **Sogdia** (/ˈsɔːgdiə/ or /ˈsɒgdiə/; Old Persian: *Suguda-*
;Ancient Greek: Σογδιανή, *Sogdianē*; Persian: سغد *Soġd*; Tajik: Суғд,
سغد *Suġd*; Uzbek: *Sugʻd*; Chinese: 粟特, Mandarin: *Sùtè*, Middle
Chinese: *Suwk-dok*) was the ancient civilization of an Iranian people and a
province of the Achaemenid Empire,

be Iranian ... *Baga* as an individual god, or the appellative *Bag*, "god",

This means that the title *"Bey"* in its original context means a divine being, or a god/goddess. The question now remains as to what sort of deities are we referring to here and what is their place in the Necronomicon Tradition History tells us that the Sogdiana who was the ancient civilization of an Iranian people and a province of the Achaemenid Persian Empire, eighteenth in the list on the Behistun Inscription of Darius the Great This seems to indicate that the Sogdians may have been descendants of the Sumerians.16

Ēl (written *aleph-lamed*,
e.g. Ugaritic: □□, Phoenician: □□, Classical
Syriac: ܐܠ, Hebrew: אל, Arabic: إل or إلٰه, cognate to Akkadian: ilu) is a Northwest Semitic word meaning "deity".

In the Canaanite religion, or Levantine religion as a whole, *El* or *Il* was a god also known as the Father of humanity and all creatures, and the husband of the goddess Asherah as recorded in the clay

---

16 Excerpt from Papers in the Attic **Hindu and Sumerian Origins Of the Title "Bey"**

: http://warlockasylum.wordpress.com/2010/09/30/hindu-and-sumerian-origins-of-the-title-bey/

tablets of Ugarit (modern *Ra's Shamrā*—Arabic: رأس شمرا, Syria). However, because the word sometimes refers to a god other than the great god Ēl, it is frequently ambiguous as to whether Ēl followed by another name means the great god Ēl with a particular epithet applied or refers to another god entirely. For example, in the Ugaritic texts, *'il mlk* is understood to mean "Ēl the King" but *'il hd* as "the god Hadad".

De or **Dey** is a surname such as Bengali, Marathi and other origins as well shared by several notable people; Surname De/Dey comes from surname Dev (Deva). They claim to be descendants of ruling Hindu classes Kayastha but in present society along with Kayastha (Alambyan gotra etc.), classses like Vaishya and Suvarna Banik can be seen. The origin of Dey/De is the subject of debate but as it is believed that they are patrilineally descended from Deva(Deb/Dev) clans of Begal.

Dey (Arabic: ياد, from Turkish *Dayı*) was the title given to the rulers of the Regency of Algiers (Algeria) and Tripoli under the Ottoman Empire from 1671 onwards. Twenty-nine *deys* held office from the establishment of the deylicate in Algeria until the French conquest in 1830.

The Dey was chosen by local civilian, military, and religious leaders to govern for life and ruled with a high degree of autonomy from the Ottoman sultan. The main sources of his revenues were taxes on the agricultural population, religious tributes, and protection payments rendered by Corsairs, regarded as pirates who preyed on Mediterranean shipping.

The dey was assisted in governing by a *divan* (ناويد) made up of the Chiefs of the Army and Navy, the Director of Shipping, the Treasurer-General and the Collector of Tributes.

Ali (Arabic: علي, *'Alī*) is a male Arabic name, derived from the Arabic root ʿ-L-Y which literally means "high" or "Elevated". It is a common name in Arabic countries and the rest of the Muslim world. Islamic traditional use of the name goes back to Ali ibn Abu Talib, the Islamic leader and cousin of Muhammad, but the name is identical in form and meaning to the Hebrew: עֵלִי , *Eli*, which goes back to the Eli in the Books of Samuel.

Al-
a word in Arabic names meaning "family" or "the house o f": *Al-Saud, or the members of the house of Saud.*
Origin:
< Arabic *āl* family

Al- (Arabic: ال, also transliterated as *el-* as pronounced in varieties of Arabic) is the definite article in the Arabic language; a particle (*ḥarf*) whose function is to render the noun on which it is prefixed definite. For example, the word تاب ك *kitāb* "book" can be made definite by prefixing it with *al-*, resulting in ال ك تاب *al-kitāb* "the book". Consequently, *al-* is typically translated as *the* in English.

The question after reading the description of names may be that these names appear to be "Turkish", Arabic or Islamic and not African. Remember that Arabic is considered part of the Afro Asiatic language. For more on this please see the book *Moors, Moabite and Man*.

CHAPTER FIVE
THE EVALUATION PLAN

The key in this exercise is to uplift Black humanity with Nationality in the city of Dayton, Ohio. The lack of proper representation and knowledge of legal, Constitutional and historical data creates a deficiency causing second-class citizenship. The perpetual downward spiral of the criminal justice system creates a virtually impossible means of success once released from prison. The lack of employment opportunities creates a backsliding in behavioral morality and a repeat offender. This is the perpetual cycle of the prison system. This has some of its roots in covert discrimination. The other point is that 13% of the "Black" population has lost their right to vote. The fight for the right to vote has been a constant struggle for the 'Black' race. This is part of the second-class citizenship clause found with the 13th Amendment.

The process to change the horrific statistics is to change the status of the African American. This process is achieved through Moorish Science

Republic of New Kemit (**MSR OF NK**). **MSR OF NK** is a body politic and civic organization, extension of Noble Drew Ali's Moorish Science Temple of America, with the primary purpose to uplift fallen humanity. The process discussed here is the process of Naturalizing or converting Black from second-class citizens into first class Citizens. The process of Naturalization is a series of classes designed to reprogram the African American from the "slave" state of mind to culturally aware National status.

INTRODUCTION TO LAW

The Law of the land is maritime and esoteric principal used by elite bankers across the world. The Law is called "business" and with corporations running multinational organizations, there is a conflict of interest with Constitutional law. The courts are now in the Jurisdiction of statutory / Maritime law.

The Moorish Republic of Kemit is striving to create an understanding and overstanding with Moors across the continent. Our goals have been to create our own Nation through our Moorish Heritage. Our other goal is assisting Blacks to re-claim their national identity regardless the religious creed.

Citizenship and our fore fathers should go hand in hand. All other ethnic groups have a root of culture that connects them to humanity and their for-fathers. Our for-father understood Law from a physical, mental and spiritual. For more overstanding of this see my book *I-Free-Ka* by Bandele Y. El-Amin.

Ultimate Law is the law of GOD. MAAT is the name used by us and our for-fathers to describe the divine law.

The law of opposites, karma and attraction originate from the womb of MAAT. This study is based on the physical laws enacted by man (physical) however, positive law is based on the Zodiac and MAAT. This is the pretext that we hold your square. Our goal is to be acknowledged by the world as a wise group of people that are lawfully conducting business.

Furthermore, this is a series of literature that will emerge as we begin to make through the matrix of ignorance that captivates our beloved children, friends and family. History, Law, economics and politics are part of the *Physical Series* dealing of the premise of the book *I Free KA*. I hope you enjoy. Bro. Bandele El

Moorish Lesson

At this point it may be necessary to expose some hidden history to some of the family, who are, or have been, by mis-education, colonial - socialization and economic conquest design, made ignorant of the vast contributions made to the world by the Moors – their Forefathers. The primes of Law and Government, most definitely, are no exception!

It has been assumed, ignorantly, by many scholars and teachers, that the savagery displayed by many of the pale-skinned descendants of Britton, who colonized the Lands of the Asiatics / Africans of the world, is representative of the ancient history of that land and its original peoples. Wrong!!! Asiatics – specifically Moors, who have also been referred to as Africans – were the early inhabitants of Britton, and were the true and original progenitors of Jurisprudence! Jurisprudence is from the Old Moorish Latin words, jurisprudentia, juris, and jus – meaning, right, law, a foreseeing, knowledge and skill. Moors also penned the primal books on the subject matters and disciplines of Jurisprudence, which are now used universally. Jurisprudence is that Science which treats of positive law and the philosophy of law. Thus, systems of law and the studies of and for the same are ancient.

The impacting, consanguine facts about Moorish History, and the true legacy of Jurisprudence, have long been known by the scholars of the world. However, due to the Inquisition and the colonization of the western hemisphere, this history has been, and is, suppressed. Now, let us refer to some definitions of the terms and phrases of American and English Jurisprudence, Ancient and Modern:

Nationality Defined; And Its Legal Status Implications

Nationality is that quality which arises from the fact of a person's belonging to a nation or state. Nationality determines the political status of the individual, especially with reference to allegiance; while domicile determines one's civil status. Nationality arises either by birth or by naturalization. Anyone who has just a minor level of knowledge of the contemporary history of North America cannot fail to recognize that persons who have born the brands of negroes, Blacks, and coloreds, etc., have traditionally suffered from status issues and the related economic and social problems emanating from the same!

The view of Nationality from a Moorish American:

Prophet Noble Drew Ali introduced `Nationalization' to the Moors of North America and instructed (the Moors) to go by, and obey, the laws of the federal, state, and county governments. This statement must be qualified by those who know law due to the fact that many, among the masses, are lacking important details of civil - liberties knowledge and of their inalienable birthrights. During that time period within the Moorish Movement (1920s) when the Prophet made that statement, the individual states of the United States of America, were Sovereign. Local and state Governments, by the Constitution law, and operated according to the states' constitutions. No state constitution was at variance to the National Constitution. The state and the federal, both, were to function (with written, delegated power limitations) according to the National Constitution for the United

States Republic. See Article VI of the Constitution. And this is the `Supreme Law of the Land'.

Counter to the Supreme Law of the Land, the form of governance for the United States Republic was, `under color', changed. This came about, progressively, after some deviant political acts took place. One of the deviant and negating political acts has come to being historically called, the `New Deal'. These acts took place under the administration of the Franklin D. Roosevelt in the year 1933. This date (1933) calculates three (3) years and eight (8) months after the Prophet Noble Drew Ali veiled his form – July 1929 A.D., shortly after he received a 50 - year mandate for the Land. This `mandate' was confirmed when Noble Drew Ali was in Cuba at the 6th Convention of the Pan-American Conference in 1928 A.D.; causing a major impact upon the wealth of North America - leading to the `New Deal' in 1933 A.D., which soon left the nation bankrupt.

The Prophet Noble Drew Ali stated in `The Divine Warning For The Nations', that "The gold, silver and commerce belongs to the Citizens alone and without your National Citizenship by name and principles, you have no true wealth, and I am, hereby, calling on all true citizens that stand for a National Free Government, and the enforcement of the Constitution to help me in my great missionary work. It is important to recognize that the Moorish tradition of instructions, commanding the enforcement of the Constitution for the United States of North America and the Territories under the jurisdiction of the United States, for all Moorish Americans and the Citizens, is paramount to understanding an important civil thrust of the Moorish Movement in North America. In consideration and review of de facto actions taken by persons occupying Seats of Government, relative to the United States, it is important to observe some of the countermeasures instituted to thwart the progressive works of Noble Drew Ali.

In the year 1933 A.D. the then presiding President, Franklin D. Roosevelt (a Master Mason) declared the nation (United States) bankrupt, and asked the Congress for `The War Powers'. Under `The War Powers Act', Roosevelt issued the Presidential Proclamation #2039. This Proclamation was issued March 6, 1933, (before Roosevelt was inaugurated a President). Logically this presented problems of unconstitutionality; and thus, Proclamation #2040; was issued March 9, 1933 (after Roosevelt took Oath to the Presidency). Thus, and upon this Proclamation, `Marshal Law' was instituted for the purpose of temporally suspending all bank transactions, and to create the guise of a suspended Constitution. Under this, Proclamation guise, `Writs of `Habeas Corpus' could and would be abused by politicians and their franchised corporate state entities. This misuse of the War Powers established *protections for racketeering persons in government, who were in opposition to the formerly secured rights of the People. The corporate States, soon after, and under the newly – established `color-of-law', adopted for themselves, `private law' for their governance, in opposition to the Constitution. These acts, in effect, were designed to neutralize the sovereignty of the `Natural Person' and to steal the birthrights-protections of the Natural People, which were secured by the `Supreme Law of the Land' - being the Constitution. This is why, in these days, the most every occupational politician of the States, the Federal and the quasi-government agencies and entities, no longer refer to the United States as `The Republic', which form of government it was confirmed as being, within the context of the Constitution. See Article IV, Section IV of the Constitution.*

Now let's take a closer look at what I understand the Mandate truly is. Drew Ali and his national cabinet. During the Pan-American Conference the Prophet Noble Drew Ali was given The Mandate for the Land, which the United States had been occupying on an expired Mandate since 1871. After this Pan American Conference of Human Nations the United States refusal to yield hallowed soil would result in a severe warning by The Holy Prophet: "Until my Moors are free in their own home the worst is yet to come. The United States owe the Moors a great debt, they must pay in compound interest. The United States have one more war to win". The next year Drew Ali left the body saying, "I can better fight the rest of this battle on the soul plane". Within twelve years of this warning the Stock Market had Crashed, Illuminati's Federal Reserve Bank had taken over the sovereign powers of the now 'Corporate United States of America' and an economical drought called "The Great Depression" was felt by every Citizen except the elite few. As if it was not enough to soften her harden heart, the US Corporation would be functioning under perpetual Maritime Law that went into effect in 1933 and has not won another War since World War II. The Prophet showed the Mandate to many Officials of the Adept Chamber of The MST of A that He founded in 1920. Still, by the year 2003, the Moors had not been redeemed from the wrath of feigned Citizenry in the USA's 14th and 15th Amendment. While the United States has never been without her staple of African Slaves, the Manumission of the Moorish is infinitely inevitable; at the end of time and the fulfilling of the prophecies.

Counter to the Supreme Law of the Land, the form of governance for the United States Republic was, 'under color', changed. This came about, progressively, after some deviant political acts took place. One of the deviant and negating political acts has come to being historically called, the 'New Deal'. These acts took place under the administration of the Franklin D. Roosevelt in the year 1933. This date (1933) calculates three (3) years and eight (8) months after the Prophet Noble Drew Ali veiled his form – July 1929 A.D., shortly after he received a 50 - year mandate for the Land. This 'mandate' was confirmed when Noble Drew Ali was in Cuba at the 6th Convention of the Pan-American Conference in 1928 A.D.; causing a major impact upon the wealth of North America - leading to the 'New Deal' in 1933 A.D., which soon left the nation bankrupt.

Noble Drew Ali lifted the veil of deception by attending the Pan American Conference in Havana, Cuba in 1928. He received extensive recognition from numerous "Heads of State" of the Americas. They recognized his sovereign status as a Moorish National who represented the Moorish Nation in the Americas. He received a copy of a mandate that extended a land grant to the "entire" Western Hemisphere" to select European nations. At that conference, the mandate for the land mass of Greater-Amexem [North, Central, and South-Central-Amexem] misnomer as the North, Central, and South "Americas" was returned to the Moors. Measures were taken by the Prophet to secure our birthright inheritance and beneficiary interest as Moors to the land mass within the aforementioned land mandate.

As I understand it land and labor is where all of your wealth comes from in the physical world and the Prophet just yanked all the land from so-called "Alaska" to so-called "Argentina" out from under them. This is the return to our place of prominence on the global scene. So the international banksters recalled all of their loans which in turn put a squeeze on their stock market which caused its collapse 2 months after the Prophet changed forms. So the European system was and is existing and functioning on borrowed time. We must reclaim all that rightly belongs to our people. We are the Moors to whom the European respective countries are tributary to as they always have been [The U.S. And Barbary Powers by David Macritchie written in the 1800's C.E. documents this fact]. The Prophet said, " What I have done is not for you Moors but for the 3rd and 4th generation from now. There will be new Moors that will come with their eyes open seeing and knowing and they will set you old Moors in the back and carry out my law".

The so-called United States, Great-Britain, France, Germany, Italy, Spain, and Portugal convened in Geneva, Switzerland for 5 continuous years [1928 C.E.-1932 C.E.] to set up what would be the policy of all of the participating countries. These 5 years of meetings became known as the Geneva-Convention. In 1930 C.E., the so-called "United States", Great-Britain, France, Germany, Italy, Spain, and Portugal all declared bankruptcy. Any *attempt to obtain the minutes of the 1930 C.E. Geneva-Convention are futile because they publish the volumes of minutes for every year of the Geneva conventions including 1930 C.E. but refuse to make the 1930 C.E. minutes available to the public because they contain the evidence of the bankruptcy.*

Going into 1932 C.E., the aforementioned states stopped meeting in Geneva. In 1932 C.E. Franklin-Roosevelt became the U.S.: President and his job was to put into place and administer the bankruptcy that the United States had declared 2 years earlier and hide the bankruptcy from the unsuspecting public by establishing a re-organization plan [The New Deal/Administrative State that functions under the "color" of the United States of America]. The United States of America and the United States for America along with the United-States: Constitution became defunct from that moment on and all that remained was the insolvent/bankrupt for profit corporation known as the United States/UNITED STATES [Codified and documented in Title 26 of the Code of Federal Regulations section 1.911-2(h), In Re Merriam 36 NE 505. 141 N.Y. 479 upheld by the 16 S. Ct 1073. 163 U.S. 625 41 L.Ed 287 See also 16 Stat 419 and District-Of-Columbia-v-Cluss 103 U.S. 705.26-1 Ed.455] operating a democratic military venue under martial law [War Powers Act] and the Uniform-Commercial-Code [Hebrew Commercial Law].

The so called States all revamped their local constitutions by 1938 C.E. to take into account their capitulation to the bankrupt mother corporation doing business as the United States thus clearing the way for the Buck Act of 1940 allowing the corporate United States to extend its jurisdiction and by default usurp all sovereignty over the now defunct State-Republics. Getting back to Roosevelt, he was sworn into the United-States: Presidency in January 1933 C.E. and wasted no time getting started with the bankruptcy. Roosevelt immediately shut the banks down [Banking Holiday] and proceeded to pull all of the gold out of circulation while replacing it with a debt currency/tender/i.o.u. with the Moors' seal [The pyramid with the all seeing eye] on the back of the U.S.: 1 dollar bill/federal reserve note.

There were eight presidents before George Washington.17 *They were in power from 1776 C.E. to 1789 C.E. George Washington was the 9th U.S. President, but the first European President and Franklin Roosevelt was the last European President to rule in that 140 year cycle. Roosevelt knew that he was the last to rule in the 144 year progressive cycle of Roman universal influence when he established a new order or new deal*

---

17 These 8 presidents were German mixed with Moors and were initiated into the Moorish mysteries.

idea and broke the Roman order by ruling for 12 years which is the measurement of man. When Roosevelt was giving those famous fireside chats, he knew what was taking place [The beginning of the gradual return of the keys of power to the rightful owners, the [Moors]. Everything that was taken from us [Moors] is quietly being prepared for its eventual return to us [Moors]; the gold [The U.S. is tributary to the Moors and they have to repay a 25 million dollars in gold loan that we made to the U.S.: Government in 1861 C.E. that the U.S.: Congress is responsible to repay which is why the seal of the Moors is on the back of the U.S. 1 dollar currency/tender/i.o.u.] and all of the land was taken and so called whites were reduced from landowner status to mere land user status. The land they murdered my ancestors for and stole so that they could fraudulently provide their silent cohorts/their people with fraudulent land grants, land patents, and allodial titles that those thieves and their descendants have no spiritual, moral, or ethical right to [The same applies in Kenya, Zimbabwe, so-called South-Africa, Australia, etc.] yet they claim they are a "God fearing nation"... If this is so, the Doctrine of Discovery from the Vatican which is still in force would cease to exist effective immediately. If this is so then the so called whites will gladly return our lands, repay the loan we made to them, make recompense to us for the Tuskegee Experiment, Emmitt Till, Maurice Bishop, The Berlin Conference, and way too much to list here [But don't worry... We will get to that too!!!] to be in harmony with the God the so called "European" claims to love, honor, respect, and obey.

The United States is bankrupt and its sovereignty is gone. The courts in the U.S. and the States are not solvent thus the Courts and Prosecutors cannot have nor bring a claim against anyone because as a bankrupt entity it has no authority to operate. Therefore the courts in the U.S. and the States cannot and will not resolve any issues. Technically, there are no more courts in the U.S. and the States. There are only private corporations doing business as quasi courts with magistrates and administrative judges (An administrative judge is not the same as a judge). The U.S. Bankruptcy is expressed in Franklin-Roosevelts' Executive Order Numbers: 6073,6111, and 6260 (See U.S. Senate Report 93-549 pp. 187, 594) under Trading With The Enemy Act of 1917 codified as United-States-Code: Title: 12: Section: 95a: House Joint Resolution 192 of June 5, 1933 C.E. confirmed in Perry-v-U.S. (1933), case site 294 U.S. 330-381 and United-States-Code: Title: 31: Sections: 5112 and 5119. United States Government are well aware of the re-emergence of the Moors on the global scene. They know that the day they or their successors return the keys of power to the original and legitimate owner, the Moors are rapidly approaching. The Moorish National, Regional, and local government will soon be on the scene and will be fully operational, and ready to govern by and under the power, authority, and permission of the Superb and Supreme Divine Creator of all things God[18].

Answer some of these very important questions to yourself.

1. Who are you in this World?
2. Are you truly free person?
3. Are you a citizen of the United States?
4. What is our Government?
5. Do you live in a "Divine" or man-made lawful world?
6. Do you live in the United States -or- the United States of America? Hmm?
7. What truly is "Identity Theft" ?
8. Am I "JOHN DOE" or am I, "John Doe" ?
9. Am I a "Person" or an "Artificial Person" ?
10. What Exactly is mail fraud?

You have taken the first step towards answering these questions and regaining your Nationality and Birthrights by reading this measure. After viewing this book, I encourage all to do your own investigating so to further educate yourself on Nationality.

---

[18] Excerpt from Milton Moore Bey.

Some have asked me why am I even doing all of this in the first place. Well I am doing all of this research and study and sharing it with all for a number of reasons. To protect, preserve and return the unalienable rights, liberties and sovereignty back to the people. To teach people that under the current system of government the people are considered Federal Citizens with granted privileges and duties, not Sovereign State Citizens with unalienable rights. To help people become better informed about the history and meaning of every provision of the Constitution and Bill of Rights. To illustrate the facts that Federal Citizenship is Statutory Slavery, that the political structure was design by the founding fathers to be a "Great Republic" not a "Democracy" and that the "United States" is foreign to the "United States of America" and lastly, to regain the sovereign rights stolen by the United States government from the people and to illustrate to the people how to recover these rights through Discovery, Realization, and Proper Assertion. So I have taken on the mission to protect, preserve and enhance the unalienable rights, liberties and freedoms of the people, to teach the people that under this system of governance all power comes from "the people" and all government is limited by the written constitutions of the people, to help the people become better informed about the history and meaning of every provision of the Declaration of Independence and their state and federal constitutions, to help the people become better informed about what is really going on in our government, to help the people become better informed about how to confront unconstitutional and illegal behavior by those wielding power in government at all levels, to reclaim the sovereignty of "the people" as you had it upon your natural birth.

The Bills Of Rights are the first ten (10) Amendments to the Constitution. The First Amendment guarantees the people certain rights respecting "Free Speech" and petitioning the government for redress of grievances. Amendment 1- Congress shall make no law respecting an establishment of religion, or prohibiting the free exercise thereof; or abridging the freedom of speech, or of the press; or the right of the people peaceably to assemble, and to petition the government for a redress of grievances.

MOORISH AMERICAN NATIONAL STATUS documentation processing from my understanding is completed when you join the MSR of NK. One you have received your Nationality packet it consists of the completion of your "Act of State and Reaffirmation" declaration, which must be witnessed and notarized, and filed with the Secretary of State for attaining an Apostille, but this process is done when the Grand Governor of that Lawfully State Chartered Temple gives you your tribal name and the Secretary of that Lawfully State Chartered Temple notarizes your ID card and gives it to you and files you as a member of that Lawfully State Chartered Temple , it is witnessed by the Grand Governor, the Secretary and all those in that Lawfully State Chartered Temple at that time.

What is an Act of State? An Act of State is a "Reaffirmation of Character and Renunciation of Attempted Expatriations". If reaffirms/reclaims your Sovereignty under the Constitution, your religion, your republic State in which you live, and you renounce and declare "VOID" any and all fictions that have been created by the government. (The ALL CAPS NAME). This gives you ABSOLUTE SOVEREIGNTY and you become the MASTER not the SLAVE (Servant). Yes, this gives you Sovereign Immunity under current United States Treaties. (23 U.S.T. 3227)

Act of State defined; "An act done by the sovereign power of a country, or by its delegate, within the limits of the power vested in him. An act of state cannot be questioned or made the subject of legal proceedings in a court of law." Black's Law Dictionary, 6th Ed., pgs 34-35

Act of State Doctrine defined: "The judicially created act of state doctrine precludes the courts of this country from inquiring into the validity of governmental acts of a recognized foreign sovereign committed within its own territory". Black's Law Dictionary, 6th Ed., pg 35.

Sovereign defined: "A person, body, or state in which independent and supreme authority is vested; a chief ruler with supreme power;" Black's Law Dictionary, 6th Ed., pg 1395.

Apostille defined: "A Standard certification provided under the Hague Convention of 1961 for purpose of authenticating documents for use in foreign countries." Black's Law Dictionary, 6th Ed., pg 96.

Most Moorish American's today are not aware that Nationality and Identification Cards of the Moorish Republic of New Kemit (A Nation State) is a Moorish American National ID Card. So this card is truly your reclaiming Common Law identity because under true law you should not have to be subject to any licensing laws, with the exception for Truck Drivers or Delivery Drivers that are employed under commercial law travel, but for private there is no requirement. Some have said that for expansion and Notices you will file your Act of State and Apostille with the U.S. District Court using general evidence records or open a Private Citizen file. It's also recommended that you file it with your states Attorney General's office and your County Sheriff's office. All you need to do from that point on is do all of your business in your tribal name of El, Dey, Ali, Al, Muhammad or Bey and put down your Nationality or make it known when and where it is necessary. So that means do everything from now on in your Free National Name. Your Nationality Card is truly for your Salvation.[19]

---

[19] Excerpt from Bro. M. Moore Bey

CHAPTER SIX
WHAT IS CITIZENSHIP?

Citizenship is membership in a political community (originally a city or town but now usually a country) and carries with it rights to political participation; a person having such membership is a **citizen**. It is largely associated with nationality although it is possible to have a nationality without being a citizen (i.e., be legally subject to a state and entitled to its protection without having rights of political participation in it); it is also possible to have political rights without being a national of a state. In most nations, a non-citizen is a non-national and called either a *foreigner* or an *alien*. In the United States, because there is state citizenship, *foreign* is the legal term for someone not a citizen of the state, and *alien* is reserved for someone not a citizen of the United States. Thus New York insurance companies are foreign in New Jersey, while a Dutch insurer is alien.

Citizenship, which is explained above, is the political rights of an individual within a society. Thus, you can have a citizenship from one country and be a national of another country. One example might be as follows: A Cuban-American might be considered a national of Cuba due to his being born there, but he could also become an American citizen through naturalization. Nationality most often derives from place of birth (i.e. *jus soli*) and, in some cases, ethnicity (i.e. *jus sanguinis*). Citizenship derives from a legal relationship with a state. Citizenship can be lost, as in denaturalization, and gained, as in naturalization.

According to 8 U.S.C. §1408[20], it is possible to be a **U.S. national** without being a U.S. citizen. A person whose

---

[20] **Section 1408.USC: Nationals but not citizens of the United States at birth**
Unless otherwise provided in section 1401 of this title, the following shall be nationals, but not citizens, of the Unites States at birth:

(1) A person born in an outlying possession of the United States on or after the date of formal acquisition of such possession;

(2) A person born outside the United States and its outlying possessions of parents both of whom are nationals, but not citizens, of the United States, and have had a residence in the United States, or one of its outlying possessions prior to the birth of such person;

(3) A person of unknown parentage found in an outlying possession of the United States while under the age of five years, until shown, prior to his attaining the age of twenty-one years, not to
have been born in such outlying possession; and

(4) A person born outside the United States and its outlying possessions of parents one of whom is an alien, and the other a national, but not a citizen, of the United States who, prior to the
Birth of such person, was physically present in the United States or its outlying possessions for a period or periods totaling not less than seven years in any continuous period of ten years -

(A) during which the national parent was not outside the United States or its outlying possessions for a continuous period of more than one year, and

(B) at least five years of which were after attaining the age
of fourteen years.
The proviso of section 1401(g) of this title shall apply to the national parent under this paragraph in the same manner as it applies to the citizen parent under that section.

only connection to the U.S. is through birth in an outlying possession (which as of 2005 is limited to American Samoa and Swains Island), or through descent from a person so born acquires U.S. nationality but not U.S. citizenship. This was formerly the case in only four other current or former U.S. overseas possessions:

Not all U.S. nationals are U.S. citizens; however, all U.S. citizens are U.S. nationals. U.S. passports normally make no distinction between the two, referring to the passport holder as a "citizen/national". Noncitizen U.S. nationals may reside and work in the United States without restrictions, and may apply for citizenship under the same rules as other resident aliens.

U.S. nationals who are not citizens and cannot vote or hold elected office at the federal level. Depending on local laws and ordinances, they may or may not be able to do so at the State or Local level.

Jus sanguinis (Latin for "right of blood") is a right by which nationality or citizenship can be recognized to any individual born to a parent who is a national or citizen of that state. It contrasts with **jus soli** (Latin for "right of soil").

At the end of the 19th century, the French-German debate on nationality saw Ernest Renan oppose the German conception of an "objective nationality", based on blood, race or even, as in Fichte's case, language. Renan's republican conception explains France's early adoption of *jus soli*. Many nations have a mixture of *jus sanguinis* and *jus soli*, including the United States, Canada, Israel, Germany (as of recently), Greece, Ireland, and others.

Apart from France, *jus sanguinis* still is the preferred means of passing on citizenship in many continental European countries, with benefits of maintaining culture and national identity as well as ethnic homogeneity. This has been criticised by some on the grounds that, if the only means, it can lead to generations of people living their whole lives in the state without being citizens of it - according to Agamben, thus likening their status to an *Homo Sacer*, deprived of any civil rights.

But notably unlike France, some European states (in their modern forms) are in fact post-empire creations within the past century. States arising out of the Austro-Hungarian and Ottoman Empires had huge numbers of ethnic populations outside of new boundaries and several had long standing diasporas inamicable to 20th century European nationalism and state creation. In many cases jus sanguinis rights were mandated by international treaty with definitions often imposed by the international community. In other cases minorities were subject to legal and extra-legal persecution and their only sage option was immigration to their ancestral home country. States offering **Jus sanguinis** rights to those persons and their descendants would include Greece, Turkey and Bulgaria all of whom are obligated by international treaty to extend those rights.

Jus soli (Latin for "right of the soil" or, somewhat figuratively, "right of the territory"), or **birthright citizenship**, is a right by which nationality or citizenship can be recognised to any individual born in the territory of the related state. At the turn of the nineteenth century, nation-states commonly divided themselves between those granting nationality on the grounds of *jus soli* (France, for example) and those granting it on the grounds of *jus sanguinis* (right of blood) (Germany, for example). However, most European countries chose the German conception of an "objective nationality", based on blood, race or language (as in Fichte's classical definition of a nation), opposing themselves to republican Ernest Renan's "subjective nationality", based on an every-day plebiscite of one's appurtenance to his Fatherland. This non-essentialist conception of nationality allowed the implementation of *jus soli*, against the essentialist *jus sanguinis*. However, today's massive increase of refugees has somewhat blurred the lines between these two antagonistic sources of right.

Body politic or **body corporate and politic** means a state or one of its subordinate civil authorities, such as a province, prefecture, county, municipality, city or district. It is generally understood to mean a geographic area with an associated government at whatever level. In previous centuries *body politic* was also understood to mean the physical person of the sovereign. (In monarchies and despotisms the person of the emperor, the king, the dictator, etc and in republics, the electorate.) It can now also mean representative of the ethnic/gender demographics of a region. For example, in many liberal democracies, cabinets are chosen to represent the body politic.

Age of majority is the threshold of adulthood as it is conceptualized in law. It is the chronological moment when children legally assume majority control over their persons and their actions and decisions, thereby terminating the legal control and legal responsibilities of their parents over and for them.

Article 15 of the Universal Declaration of Human Rights states:

1. Everyone has the right to a nationality.

2. No one shall be arbitrarily deprived of his nationality nor denied the right to change his nationality.

Today, nationality law is based either on jus soli or jus sanguinis, or on a combination of the two. Jus soli is the principle in which a child born in a country's territorial jurisdiction acquires that country's nationality (Ex: United States, Canada, Argentina, Brazil, Mexico, France [including in its overseas dependencies]). In jus sanguinis, either the father or mother must normally be a citizen of the country in question in order for the child to be a citizen (e.g. Israel, Switzerland).

A **native-born citizen** of a country is a person who is legally recognized as that country's citizen at the moment of birth and was also born within that country.

A person can be considered to be a "citizen-at-birth" either due to place of birth within that country's territorial jurisdiction (jus soli) or through descent from a citizen of that country (jus sanguinis), or through some combination of those two elements. A person who is a "citizen-at-birth" and was also born within that country would be additionally considered a "native-born citizen".

It should be noted that a person that inherited citizenship through an ancestor but was born outside the country of citizenship would be considered a "citizen-at-birth" [Moors in America] (rather than a naturalized citizen) but would not be considered a "native-born citizen". Furthermore, a person who was born in a country that did not recognize him as its citizen at birth but later naturalized as its citizen would also not be considered a "native-born citizen".[21]

In many countries (including Japan), a native-born individual may not be a citizen. Sadaharu Oh is not a Japanese citizen despite being born in Japan and having a Japanese mother.

In some countries, such as the United States, native birth is a requirement for certain high offices, such as the head of state.

Although the U.S. Supreme Court has never specifically addressed the meaning of "natural born citizen," there are several Supreme Court decisions that help define citizenship:

- *Dred Scott v. Sandford,* 60 U.S. 393 (1857): In regard to the "natural born citizen" clause, the dissent states that it is acquired by place of birth (*jus soli*), not through blood or lineage (*jus sanguinis*): "The first section of the second article of the Constitution uses the language, 'a natural-born citizen.' It thus assumes that citizenship may be acquired by birth. Undoubtedly, this language of the Constitution was used in reference to that principle of public law, well

---

21 This is an example of blacks' and the 14th Amendment.

understood in this country at the time of the adoption of the Constitution, which referred citizenship to the place of birth." (The majority opinion in this case was mostly overturned by the 14th Amendment.)

- *United States v. Wong Kim Ark,* 169 U.S. 649 (1898): A person born within the jurisdiction of the U.S. to non-citizens who "are not employed in any diplomatic or official capacity" is automatically a citizen.
- *Weedin v. Chin Bow,* 274 U.S. 657 (1927): A child born outside the U.S. cannot claim U.S. citizenship by birth through a U.S. citizen parent who had never lived in the U.S. prior to the child's birth. (This is still true today, although the specific statutes upon which the Supreme Court's ruling was based have changed since 1927.)
- *Perez v. Brownell,* 356 U.S. 44 (1958): Although the 14th Amendment sets forth the two principal modes of acquiring citizenship (birth in the U.S. and naturalization), nothing restricts the power of Congress to withdraw citizenship. (This case was overturned by *Afroyim v. Rusk.*)
- *Montana v. Kennedy,* 366 U.S. 308 (1961): A person born in 1906, whose mother was a native-born citizen of the United States and whose father was a foreign citizen, who was born overseas and then moved to the United States, was not a citizen of the United States by birth. (Note that the relevant laws have

changed considerably since 1906, so this decision does not necessarily apply to later cases.)

- *Afroyim v. Rusk,* 387 U.S. 253 (1967): The 14th Amendment's provision that "All persons born or naturalized in the United States . . . are citizens of the United States" completely controls the status of citizenship and prevents the involuntary cancellation of citizenship.

- *Rogers v. Bellei,* 401 U.S. 815 (1971): A person who is born abroad to an American mother shall lose his or her citizenship unless he or she resides in this country for at least five years between the ages of 14 and 28. (This is no longer the case; the statute under which Mr. Bellei lost his citizenship was repealed by Congress in 1978.)

- *Vance v. Terrazas,* 444 U.S. 252 (1980): Congress has the power to define acts of expatriation (i.e., loss of citizenship). However, intent to relinquish U.S. citizenship must be established specifically by a preponderance of evidence; such an intent may not be inferred automatically as a result of a person's having performed an act which Congress has designated as an expatriating act. However, when "one of the statutory expatriating acts is proved, it is constitutional to presume it to have been a voluntary act until and unless proved otherwise by the actor."

- *Miller v. Albright,* 523 U.S. 420 (1998): A child born overseas to an American father and a foreign mother (not married) is not a U.S. citizen unless paternity is established before an established age (in this case 21). This case challenged the law on the grounds that U.S. law requires no explicit acknowledgment of parenthood in the case of a foreign-born child to an American mother and a foreign father (not married).

- *Nguyen v. INS,* 533 U.S. 53 (2001): As in the *Miller v. Albright* case, the Court holds that a child born overseas to an American father and a foreign mother (not married) is not a U.S. citizen unless paternity is established before an established age (in this case 18). The child was brought to the U.S. before his sixth birthday and raised by his father; however, after a criminal conviction, deportation was ordered but the child claimed U.S. citizenship. His citizenship was denied because paternity had not been established prior to his 18th birthday. The Court upheld the law, once again affirming that Congress has the power to define citizenship outside the citizenship dictated by the 14th Amendment (citizenship by birth).

The Supreme Court, through case law, has created a guideline for U.S. citizenship. The following outlines the rulings of the Court:

- The 14th Amendment completely controls the status of U.S. citizenship and prevents the involuntary cancellation of citizenship.
  - All persons born in the United States are citizens of the United States.
    - This applies to children born to legal and illegal residents.
    - This does not apply to children of foreign citizens employed in any diplomatic or official capacity.
  - Congress has the power to define acts of expatriation (i.e., loss of citizenship).
    - A person must voluntarily relinquish U.S. citizenship.
      - It is constitutional to presume it to have been a voluntary act until and unless proved otherwise by the actor.
      - Congress may revoke citizenship involuntarily if it has been obtained unlawfully.
- Congress has the power to define citizenship outside birth in the U.S.
  - Congress can set different citizenship requirements for children born to American mothers versus American fathers.
  - Congress can require that U.S. citizenship must be established by a certain age for it to be recognized.

Domicile

In Conflict of Laws, **domicile** (termed **domicil** in the U.S.) is the basis of the choice of law rule operating in the characterization framework to define a person's status, capacity and rights. The international term for this as a connecting factor is the *lex domicilii*, i.e. the law of the domicile.

Domicile should also be clearly distinguished from nationality (also known as *lex patriae*) which is the relationship between an individual and a country. Where the state and the country are co-extensive, the two are the same. But where the country is federated into separate legal systems, nationality and domicile will be different. Hence, one might have American nationality and a domicile in Texas. Further, one can have dual nationality but not more than one domicile at a time. This does not prevent a person from having a domicile in one state while maintaining nationality in another country. Unlike nationality, no person can be without a domicile even if stateless. Domicile is being supplanted by habitual residence in the international conventions dealing with Conflict and other private law matters.

A person who has reached the age of majority, is free to choose a new domicile. This choice is effective when an individual has both:

1. the *factum*, i.e. unequivocally abandons the old domicile, and
2. the *animus semper manendi*, i.e. enters a new state with the intent to make it their permanent home.

The latter is very difficult to prove because most people retain affection for their previous state and think that they may one day return. Even if a domicile of choice is found to have arisen, it will be lost as soon as either the *factum* or the *animus* is lost. At this point, the domicile of origin revives

Each State of the United States is considered a separate sovereign within the U.S. federal system, and each therefore has its own laws on questions of marriage, inheritance, and liability for tort and contract actions. Persons who reside the U.S. must have a state domicile for various purposes. For example, an individual can always be sued in their state of domicile. Furthermore, in order for parties to invoke the diversity jurisdiction of a United States Federal Court, the plaintiffs may not have the same domicile as any defendant.

COMMON LAW

In **common law** legal systems, the law is created and/or refined by judges: a decision in the case currently pending depends on decisions in previous cases and affects the law to be applied in future cases. When there is no authoritative statement of the law, common law judges have the authority and duty to "make" law by creating precedent. The body of precedent is called "common law" and it binds future decisions. In future cases, when parties disagree on what the law is, an "ideal" common law court looks to past precedential decisions of relevant courts. If a similar dispute has been resolved in the past, the court is bound to follow the reasoning used in the prior decision (this principle is known as *stare decisis*). If, however, the court finds that the current dispute is fundamentally distinct from all previous cases, it will decide as a "matter of first impression." Thereafter, the new decision becomes precedent, and will bind future courts under the principle of *stare decisis*.

In practice, common law systems are considerably more complicated than the "ideal" system described above. The decisions of a court are binding only in a particular jurisdiction, and even within a given jurisdiction, some courts have more power than others. For example, in most jurisdictions, decisions by appellate courts are binding on lower courts in the same jurisdiction and on future decisions of the same appellate court, but decisions of non-appellate courts are only non-binding persuasive authority. Interactions between common law, constitutional law, statutory law and regulatory law also give rise to considerable complexity. However *stare decisis*, the principle that similar cases should be decided according to similar rules, lies at the heart of all common law systems.

Common law legal systems are in widespread use, particularly in those nations which trace their legal heritage to Britain, including the United Kingdom, most of the United States and Canada, and other former colonies of the British Empire.

There are three main connotations to the term **common law**, and several historical ones worth mentioning:

1. Common law as opposed to statutory law and regulatory law

This connotation distinguishes the authority that promulgated a law. For example, in most areas of law in most jurisdictions in the United States, there are "statutes" enacted by a legislature, "regulations" promulgated by executive branch agencies pursuant to a delegation of rule-making authority from a legislature, and common law or "case law", i.e. decisions issued by courts (or quasi-judicial tribunals within agencies). This first connotation can be further differentiated, into (a) laws that arise purely from the common law with no express statutory authority, e.g. most criminal law and procedural law before the 20th century, and even today, most of contract law and the law of torts, and (b) decisions that discuss and decide the fine boundaries and distinctions in written laws promulgated by other bodies, such as the Constitution, statutes and regulations. See statutory law and non-statutory law.

2. Common law legal systems as opposed to civil law legal systems

This connotation differentiates "common law" jurisdictions and legal systems from "civil law" or "code" jurisdictions. Common law systems place great weight on court decisions, which are considered "law" just as are statutes. By contrast, in civil law jurisdictions (the legal tradition that prevails in, or is combined with common law, in almost all non-Islamic, non-common law countries), judicial precedent is given less weight, and contributions by scholars are also considered. For example, the Napoleonic code expressly forbade French judges from pronouncing the law.

3. Law as opposed to equity

This connotation differentiates "common law" (or just "law") from "equity". Before 1873, England had two parallel court systems: courts of "law" that could only award money damages and recognized only the legal owner of property, and courts of "equity" that could issue injunctive relief and recognized trusts of property. This split propagated many of the colonies, including the United States (see "Reception Statutes," below). The distinction between "law" and "equity" was important in: (a) categorizing and prioritizing rights to property; (b) in the United States, determining whether the Seventh Amendment's right to a jury trial applies (a determination of a fact necessary to resolution of a "common law" claim) or whether the issue may be decided by a judge (issues of what the law is, and all issues relating to equity); and (c) in the principles that apply to the grant of equitable remedies by the courts. For most purposes, most jurisdictions, including those within the US, have merged the two courts. Additionally, even before the separate courts were merged together, most courts were permitted to apply both law and equity (though under potentially different laws of procedure). Even so, the split survives and remains relevant for determining at least these three classes of issues. Other exceptions are discussed in "Common Law Systems," below.

4. Historical uses

In addition, there are several historical uses of the term that provide some background as to its meaning. The English Court of Common Pleas dealt with lawsuits in which the king had no interest, i.e. between commoners. Additionally, from at least the 11th century and continuing for several centuries after that, there were several different circuits in the royal court system, served by itinerant judges who would travel from town to town dispensing the King's justice. The term "common law" was used to describe the law held in common between the circuits and the different stops in each circuit. The more widely a particular law was recognized, the more weight it held, whereas purely local customs were generally subordinate to law recognized in a plurality of jurisdictions. These definitions are archaic, their relevance having dissipated with the development of the English legal system over the centuries, but they do explain the origin of the term.

Basic principles of common law

Common law adjudication

In a common law jurisdiction, several stages of research and analysis are required to determine what "the law is" in a given situation. First, one must ascertain the facts. Then, one must locate any relevant statutes and cases. Then one must extract the principles, analogies and statements by various courts of what they consider important to determine how the next court is likely to rule on the facts of the present case. Later decisions, and decisions of higher courts or legislatures carry more weight than earlier cases and those of lower courts.[4] Finally, one integrates all the lines drawn and reasons given, and determines what "the law is". Then, one applies that law to the facts.

The common law is more malleable than statutory law. First, common law courts are not absolutely bound by precedent, but can (when extraordinarily good reason is shown) reinterpret and revise the law, without legislative intervention, to adapt to new trends in political, legal and social philosophy. Second, the common law evolves through a series of gradual steps, that gradually works out all the details, so that over a decade or more, the law can change substantially but without a sharp break, thereby reducing disruptive effects. In contrast, the legislative process is very difficult to get started: legislatures do not act until a situation is totally intolerable. Because of this, legislative changes tend to be large, jarring and disruptive (either positively or negatively).

One example of the gradual change that typifies the common law is the gradual change in liability for negligence. For example, the traditional common law rule through most of the 19th century was that a plaintiff could not recover for a defendant's negligence unless the two were in privity of contract. Thus, only the immediate purchaser could recover for a product defect, and if a part was built up out of parts from parts manufacturers, the ultimate buyer could not recover for injury caused by a defect in the part. *Winterbottom v. Wright*, 10 M&W 109, 152 Eng.Rep. 402, 1842 WL 5519 (Exchequer of pleas 1842). In *Winterbottom*, the postal service had contracted with Wright to maintain its coaches. Winterbottom was a driver for the post. When the coach failed and injured Winterbottom, he sued Wright. The *Winterbottom* court recognized that there would be "absurd and outrageous consequences" if an injured person could sue any person peripherally involved, but could not find a good place to draw a line around the causal connection between the negligent conduct and the injury other than to limit liability to only the immediate person in contract with the negligent party. A first exception to this rule arose in *Thomas v. Winchester*, 6 N.Y. 397 (N.Y. 1852) which held that mislabeling a poison as an innocuous herb, and then selling the mislabeled poison through a dealer who would be expected to resell it, put "human life in imminent danger." *Thomas* used this as a reason to create an exception to the "privity" rule. In *Statler v. Ray Mfg. Co.*, 195 N.Y. 478, 480 (N.Y. 1909) held that a coffee urn manufacturer was liable to a person injured when the urn exploded, because the urn "was of such a character inherently that, when applied to the purposes for which it was designed, it was liable to become a source of great danger to many people if not carefully and properly constructed."

Yet the privity rule survived. In *Cadillac Motor Car Co. v Johnson*, 221 F. 801 (2nd Cir. 1915) (decided by the federal appeals court for New York and several neighboring states), the court held that a car owner could not recover for injuries from a defective wheel, when the automobile owner only had a contract with the automobile dealer, not with the manufacturer, even though there was "no question that the wheel was made of dead and 'dozy' wood, quite insufficient for its purposes."

Finally, in the famous case of *MacPherson v. Buick Motor Co.*, 217 N.Y. 382, 111 N.E. 1050 (N.Y. 1916), Judge Cardozo pulled a broader principle out of these predecessor cases. The facts were almost identical to *Cadillac* a year earlier: a wheel from a wheel manufacturer was sold to Buick, to a dealer, to MacPherson, and the wheel failed, injuring MacPherson. Judge Cardozo held:

> We hold, then, that the principle of *Thomas v. Winchester* is not limited to poisons, explosives, and things of like nature, to things which in their normal operation are implements of destruction. If the nature of a thing is such that it is reasonably certain to place life and limb in peril when negligently made, it is

then a thing of danger. Its nature gives warning of the consequences to be expected. If to the element of danger there is added knowledge that the thing will be used by persons other than the purchaser, and used without new tests then, irrespective of contract, the manufacturer of this thing of danger is under a duty to make it carefully. ... There must be knowledge of a danger, not merely possible, but probable.

Note that Cardozo's new "rule" exists in no prior case, but is inferable as a synthesis of the principles stated in them, and represents a foreseeable progression. Importantly, note that Judge Cardozo continues to adhere to the original principle of *Winterbottom*, that "absurd and outrageous consequences" must be avoided, and he does so by drawing a new line in the last sentence quoted above: "There must be knowledge of a danger, not merely possible, but probable." But while adhering to the underlying principle, *MacPherson* overruled the rule of the prior common law by stating that privity was irrelevant.

Interaction of constitutional, statute and common law

In common law legal systems, the common law is crucial to understanding almost all important areas of law. For example, in England and Wales and in most states of the United States, the basic laws of contracts, torts and property do not exist in statute, but only in common law (though there may be isolated modifications enacted by statute). In almost all areas of the law (even those where there is a statutory framework, such as contracts for the sale of goods, or the criminal law), other written laws generally give only terse statements of general principle, and the fine boundaries and definitions exist only in the common law. To find out what the precise law is that applies to a particular set of facts, one has to locate precedential decisions on the topic, and reason from those decisions by analogy. To consider but one example, the First Amendment to the United States Constitution states "Congress shall make no law respecting an establishment of religion, or prohibiting the free exercise thereof" – but interpretation (that is, determining the fine boundaries, and resolving the tension between the "establishment" and "free exercise" clauses) of each of the important terms was delegated by Article III of the Constitution to the judicial branch, so that the current legal boundaries of the Constitutional text can only be determined by consulting the common law.

In common law jurisdictions, legislatures operate under the assumption that statutes will be interpreted against the backdrop of the pre-existing common law case law and custom, and so may leave a number of things unsaid. For example, in most U.S. states, the criminal statutes are primarily codification of pre-existing common law. (Codification is the process of enacting a statute that collects and restates pre-existing law in a single document when that pre-existing law is common law, the common law remains relevant to the interpretation of these statutes.) In reliance on this assumption, modern statutes often leave a number of terms and fine distinctions unstated -- for example, a statute might be very brief, leaving the precise definition of terms unstated, under the assumption that these fine distinctions will be inherited from pre-existing common law. For this reason, even today American law schools teach the common law of crime as practiced in England in 1789, because the backdrop of centuries-old English common law is necessary to interpret and fully understand the literal words of the modern criminal statute.

With the transition from English law, which had common law crimes, to the new legal system under the U.S. Constitution, which prohibited ex post facto laws at both the federal and state level, the question was raised whether there could be common law crimes in the United States. It was settled in the case of *United States v. Hudson and Goodwin* which decided that common law crimes were prohibited (at least at the Federal level), and that there must always be a (constitutional) statute defining the offense and the penalty for it.

By contrast to the statutory codifications of common law, some laws are purely statutory, and may create a new cause of action beyond the common law. An example is the tort of wrongful death, which allows certain persons, usually a spouse, child or estate, to sue for damages on behalf of the deceased. There is no such tort in English common law; thus, any jurisdiction that lacks a wrongful death statute will not allow a lawsuit for the wrongful death of a loved one. Where a wrongful death statute exists, the compensation or other remedy available is limited to the remedy specified in the statute (typically, an upper limit on the amount of damages). Courts generally interpret statutes that create new causes of action narrowly – that is, limited to their precise terms – because the courts generally recognize the legislature as being supreme in deciding the reach of judge-made law unless such statute should violate some "second order" constitutional law provision (*cf.* judicial activism).

Where a tort is rooted in common law, then all traditionally recognized damages for that tort may be sued for, whether or not there is mention of those damages in the current statutory law. For instance, a person who sustains bodily injury through the negligence of another may sue for medical costs, pain, suffering, loss of earnings or earning capacity, mental and/or emotional distress, loss of quality of life, disfigurement and more. These damages need not be set forth in statute as they already exist in the tradition of common law. However, without a wrongful death statute, most of them are extinguished upon death.

Contrasting role of treatises and academic writings in common law and civil law systems

In many subject matter areas, legal treatises compile common law decisions, and state overarching principles that (in the author's opinion) explain the results of the cases. However, in common law jurisdictions, treatises are not the law, and lawyers and judges tend to use these treatises as only "finding aids" to locate the relevant cases.

This is one of the "cultural" differences between common law and civil law jurisdictions (connotation 2): in civil law jurisdictions, the writings of law professors are given significant weight by courts. In common law jurisdictions, scholarly work is seldom cited as authority for what the law is. When common law courts rely on scholarly work, it is almost always only for factual findings, policy justification, or the history and evolution of the law, but the court's legal conclusion is reached through analysis of relevant statutes and common law, seldom scholarly commentary.

Common law as a foundation for commercial economies

This reliance on judicial opinion is a strength of common law systems, and is a significant contributor to the robust commercial systems in the United Kingdom and United States. Because there is common law to give reasonably precise guidance on almost every issue, parties (especially commercial parties) can predict whether a proposed course of action is likely to be lawful or unlawful. This ability to predict gives more freedom to come close to the boundaries of the law. For example, many commercial contracts are more economically efficient, and create greater wealth, because the parties know ahead of time that the proposed arrangement, though perhaps close to the line, is almost certainly legal. Newspapers, taxpayer-funded entities with some religious affiliation, and political parties can obtain fairly clear guidance on the boundaries within which their freedom of expression rights apply. In contrast, in non-common-law countries, fine questions of law are re determined anew each time they arise, making consistency and prediction more difficult. Thus, in jurisdictions that do not have a strong allegiance to a large body of precedent, parties have less *a priori* guidance must often leave a bigger "safety margin" of unexploited opportunities.

This is the reason for the frequent choice of the law of the State of New York in commercial contacts from throughout the United States. In particular, English law and New York law are often used in contracts throughout the world, even where the relationship of the contact parties and transaction to England or New York is quite attenuated. Because of its history as the nation's commercial center, English and New York common law have a depth and predictability not (yet) available in any other jurisdiction.

In common law systems, conflict of laws, firstly, is concerned with determining whether the proposed forum has jurisdiction to adjudicate and is the appropriate venue for dealing with the dispute, and, secondly, with determining which of the competing state's laws are to be applied to resolve the dispute. It also deals with the enforcement of foreign judgments.

Civil law (legal system)

Civil law or *Romano-Germanic law* or *Continental law* is the predominant system of law in the world, in which an abstract code of law rules, which judges apply to the various cases before them. It is often distinguished from common law, in which abstract rules are derived from specific cases.

Civil law has its roots in Roman law, Canon law (Christian, especially Catholic law) and the Enlightenment, alongside influences from other religious laws such as Islamic law. The legal systems in many civil law countries are based around one or several codes of law, which set out the main principles that guide the law. The most famous example is perhaps the French Civil Code, although the German Bürgerliches Gesetzbuch (or BGB) and the Swiss Civil Code are also landmark events in the history of civil law. The civil law systems of Scotland and South Africa are uncodified, and the civil law systems of Scandinavian countries remain largely uncodified. The so-called Socialist law is often considered to be a particular case of the Romano-Germanic civil law, though in the past it was sometimes classified as a separate legal system.

Civil versus Common law

Civil law is primarily contrasted against common law, which is the legal system developed among Anglophone people, especially in England.

The original difference is that, historically, common law was law developed by custom, beginning before there were any written laws and continuing to be applied by courts after there were written laws, too, whereas civil law developed out of the Roman law of Justinian's Corpus Juris Civilis (*Body of Civil Law*).

In later times, civil law became codified as *droit coutumier* or customary law that were local compilations of legal principles recognized as normative. Sparked by the age of enlightenment, attempts to codify private law began during the second half of the 18th century (*see* civil code), but civil codes with a lasting influence were promulgated only after the French Revolution, in jurisdictions such as France (with its Napoleonic Code), Austria (*see* ABGB), Quebec (*see* Civil Code of Quebec), Italy (Codice Civile), Portugal (Código Civil), Spain (Código Civil), the Netherlands (*see* Burgerlijk Wetboek), and Germany (*see* Bürgerliches Gesetzbuch). However, codification is by no means a defining characteristic of a civil law system, as e.g. the civil law systems of Scandinavian countries remain largely uncodified, whereas common law jurisdictions have frequently codified parts of their laws, e.g. in the U.S. Uniform Commercial Code. There are also mixed systems, such as the laws of Scotland, Louisiana, Quebec, the Philippines, Namibia and South Africa.

Thus, the difference between civil law and common law lies not just in the mere fact of codification, but in the methodological approach to codes and statutes. In civil law countries, legislation is seen as the primary source of law. By default, courts thus base their judgments on the provisions of codes and statutes, from which solutions in particular cases are to be derived. Courts thus have to reason extensively on the basis of general rules and principles of the code, often drawing analogies from statutory provisions to fill lacunae and to achieve coherence. By contrast, in the common law system, cases are the primary source of law, while statutes are only seen as incursions into the common law and thus interpreted narrowly.

The underlying principle of separation of powers is seen somewhat differently in civil law and common law countries. In some common law countries, especially the United States, judges are seen as balancing the power of the other branches of government. By contrast, the original idea of separation of powers in France was to assign different roles to legislation and to judges, with the latter only applying the law (the judge as *la bouche de la loi*; 'the mouth of the law'). This translates into the fact that many civil law jurisdictions reject the formalistic notion of binding precedent (although paying due consideration to settled case-law), or restrict the power to set precedents to a competent Supreme Court.

Uniform Commercial Code

The **Uniform Commercial Code** (**UCC** or the Code) is one of a number of uniform acts that have been promulgated in conjunction with efforts to harmonize the law of sales and other commercial transactions in all 50 states within the United States of America. This objective is deemed important because of the prevalence today of commercial transactions that extend beyond one state (for example, where the goods are manufactured in state A, warehoused in state B, sold from state C and delivered in state D). The UCC deals primarily with transactions involving personal property (movable property), not real property (immovable property).

The UCC is the longest and most elaborate of the uniform acts. It has been a long-term, joint project of the National Conference of Commissioners on Uniform State Laws (NCCUSL) and the American Law Institute (ALI). Judge Herbert F. Goodrich was the Chairman of the Editorial Board of the original 1952 edition, and the Code itself was drafted by some of the top legal scholars in the United States, including Karl N. Llewellyn, William A.

Schnader, Soia Mentschikoff, and Grant Gilmore. The Code, as the product of private organizations, is not itself the law, but only recommendation of the laws that should be adopted in the states. Once enacted in a state by the state's legislature, it becomes true law and is codified into the state's code of statutes. When the Code is adopted by a state, it may be adopted verbatim as written by ALI and NCCUSL, or may be adopted with specific changes deemed necessary by the state legislature. Unless such changes are minor, they can affect the purpose of the Code in promoting uniformity of law among the various states.

CHAPTER SEVEN
DRED SCOT

This is the inhumane process that Moors had to encounter as Negro, Colored and Black. The *Dred Scott* case would be the precedent set into motion the status that "Blacks" still are under!

Excerpts from the
Dred Scott Supreme Court Decision
Mr. Justice Daniel presiding, December Term, 1856.
DRED SCOTT, PLAINTIFF IN ERROR, V. JOHN F. SANDFORD

I.

4. A free Negro of the African race, whose ancestors were brought to this country and sold as slaves, is not a "citizen" within the meaning of the Constitution of the United States.

When the constitution was adopted, they were not regarded in any of the States as members of the community which constituted the State, and were not numbered among its "people or citizens." Consequently, the special rights and immunities guaranteed to citizens do not apply to them.

Section 2

The words "people of the united States" and "citizens" are synonymous terms, and mean the same thing. They both describe the political body who, according to our republican institutions, form the sovereignty, and who hold the power and conduct the Government through their representatives. They are what we familiarly call the "sovereign people," and every citizen is one of this people, and a constituent member of this sovereignty. The question before us is, whether the class of persons described in the plea in abatement compose a portion of this people, and are constituent members of this sovereignty? We think they are not, and they are not included, and were not intended to be included, under the word "citizens" in the constitution, and can therefore claim none of the rights and privileges which that instrument provides for and secures to citizens of the United States. On the contrary, they were at that time considered as a subordinate and inferior class of beings, who had been subjugated by the dominant race, and, whether emancipated or not, yet remained subject to their authority, and have no rights or privileges but such as those who held the power and the Government might choose to grant them.

DECEMBER TERM, 1856. 407

DRED SCOTT V. SANDFORD - Opinion of the Court

Section 4

They had for more than a century before been regarded as beings of an inferior order, and altogether unfit to associate with the white race, either in social or political relations; and so far inferior, that they had no rights which the white man was bound to respect.

DECEMBER TERM, 1856. 406

OPINION OF THE COURT - Dred Scott v. Sandford.

Section 3

It is true, every person, and every class and description of persons, who were at the time of the adoption of the Constitution recognized as citizens in the several States, become also citizens of this new political body; but none other; it was formed by them, and for them and their posterity, but for no one else. And the personal rights and privileges guaranteed to citizens of this new sovereignty were intended to embrace those only who were then members of the several State communities, or who should afterwards by birthright or otherwise become members, according to the provisions of the Constitution and the principles on which it was founded.. It was the union of those who were at that time members of distinct and separate political communities into one political family, whose power, for certain specified purposes, was to extend over the whole territory of the United States.

DECEMBER TERM, 1856.

Dred Scott v. Sandford MR. JUSTICE DANIEL

Page 475, section 2

*Now, the following are truths which a knowledge of the history of the world, and particularly of that of our own country, compels us to know–that **the African Negro race never have been acknowledged as belonging to the family of nations; that as amongst them there never has been known or recognized by the inhabitants of other countries anything partaking of the character of nationality, or civil or political polity; that this race has been by all the nations of Europe regarded as subjects of capture or purchase.***

DECEMBER TERM, 1856. 407

Dred Scott v. Sandford - Opinion of the Court

It is difficult at this day to realize the state of public opinion in relation to that unfortunate race, which prevailed in the civilized and enlightened portions of the world at the time of the Declaration of Independence.

Page 476, Section 2

For who, it may be asked, what is a citizen ? What do the character and status of citizen import? Without fear of contradiction, it does not import the condition of being private property, the subject of individual power and ownership. Upon a principle of etymology alone, the term citizen, as derived from civitas, conveys the ideas of connection or identification with the State or Government, and a participation of its functions. But beyond this, there is not, it is believed, to be found, in the theories of writers on Government, or in any actual experiment heretofore tried, an exposition of the term citizen, which has not been understood as conferring the actual possession and enjoyment, or the perfect right of acquisition and enjoyment, of an entire equality of privileges, civil and political.

Thus Vattel, in the preliminary chapter to his Treatise on the Law of Nations, says: " Nations or States are bodies politic; societies of men united together for the purpose of promoting their mutual safety and advantage, by the joint efforts of their mutual strength. Such a society has her affairs and her interests; she deliberates and takes resolutions in common; thus becoming a moral person, who possesses an understanding and a will peculiar to herself."

Again, in the first chapter of the first book of the Treatise just quoted, the same writer, after repeating his definition of a State, proceeds to remark, that, "from the very design that induces a number of men to form a society, which has its common interests and which is to act in concert, it is necessary that there should be established a public authority, to order and direct what is to be done by each, in relation to the end of the association.

This political authority is the Sovereignty." Again this writer remarks: "The authority of all over each member essentially belongs to the body politic or the State." By this same writer it is also said: "The citizens are the members of the civil society; bound to this society by certain duties, and subject to its authority; they equally participate in its advantages. The natives, or natural-born citizens, are those born in the country, of parents who are citizens. As society cannot perpetuate itself otherwise then by the children of the citizens, those children naturally follow the condition of their parents, and succeed to all their rights."

Page 481, Section 2

The first, and to my mind a conclusive reply to this singular argument is presented in the fact, that the language of the Constitution restricts the jurisdiction of the courts to cases in which the parties shall be citizens, and is entirely silent with respect to residence. A second answer to this strange and latitudinous notion is, that it so far stultifies the sages by whom the Constitution was framed, as to impute to them ignorance of the material distinction existing between citizenship and mere **residence or domicile**, and of the well-known facts, that a person confessedly an alien may be permitted to reside in a country in which he can possess no civil or political rights, or of which he is neither a citizen nor subject; and that for certain purposes a man may have a domicile in different countries, in no one of which he is an actual personal resident.

The correct conclusions upon the question here considered would seem to be these: That in the establishment of the several communities now the States of this Union, and in the formation of the Federal Government, the African was not deemed politically a person. He was regarded and owned in every State in the Union as property merely, and as such was not and could not be a party or an actor, much less a peer in any compact or form of government established by the

States or the United States. That if, since the adoption of the State Governments, he has been or could have been elevated to the possession of political rights or powers, this result could have been effected by no authority less potent than that of the sovereignty -- the State--exerted to that end, either in the form of legislation, or in some other mode of operation. It could certainly never have been accomplished by the will of an individual operating independently of the sovereign power, and even contravening and controlling that power. That so far as rights and immunities appertaining to citizens have been defined and secured by the Constitution and laws of the United States, the African race is not and never was recognized either by the language or purposes of the former; and it has been expressly excluded by every act of Congress providing for the creation of citizens by naturalization, these laws, as has already been remarked, being restricted to free white aliens exclusively.

But it is evident that, after the formation of the Federal Government by the adoption of the Constitution, the highest exertion of State power would be incompetent to bestow a character or status created by the Constitution, or conferred in virtue of its authority only. Upon those, therefore, who were not originally parties to the Federal compact, or who are not admitted and adopted as parties thereto, in the mode prescribed by its paramount authority, no State could have power to bestow the character or the rights and privileges exclusively reserved by the States for the action of the Federal Government by that compact.

Rates of Incarceration by Race, 1996

State/Black/White/Ratio   States   Ranked   By
Black/White

State	Black	White	Ratio		State	Ratio
ALABAMA	1271	236	5		DC	34
ALASKA	2223	388	6		MINNESOTA	23
ARIZONA	2134	441	5		IOWA	18
ARKANSAS	1268	200	6		WISCONSIN	17
CALIFORNIA	1909	168	11		CONNECTICUT	17
COLORADO	1794	241	7		PENNSYLVANIA	16
CONNECTICUT	2296	139	17		ILLINOIS	14
DELAWARE	2340	302	8		NEW JERSEY	13
DC	2720	81	34		TEXAS	12
FLORIDA	1574	223	7		CALIFORNIA	11
GEORGIA	1111	219	5		NEBRASKA	11
HAWAII	579	219	3		RHODE ISLAND	11
IDAHO	951	265	4		UTAH	11
ILLINOIS	1395	98	14		KANSAS	10
INDIANA	1480	183	8		OHIO	9
IOWA	2818	159	18		MASSACHUSETTS	9
KANSAS	1947	191	10		MARYLAND	9
KENTUCKY	1692	225	8		OREGON	9
LOUISIANA	1480	210	7		WASHINGTON	8
MARYLAND	1225	140	9		NEW HAMPSHIRE	8
MASSACHUSETTS	907	101	9		INDIANA	8
MICHIGAN	1695	212	8		MICHIGAN	8
MINNESOTA	1383	59	23		VIRGINIA	8
MISSISSIPPI	1040	203	5		WYOMING	8
MISSOURI	1702	245	7		DELAWARE	8

MONTANA 1589 219 7
NEBRASKA 1536 137 11
NEVADA 1829 325 6
NEW HAMPSHIRE 1373 168 8
NEW JERSEY 1526 115 13
NEW MEXICO 1259 261 5
NEW YORK 1172 216 5
NORTH CAROLINA 1218 171 7
NORTH DAKOTA 571 88 6
OHIO 1964 213 9
OKLAHOMA 2681 384 7
OREGON 1826 212 9
PENNSYLVANIA 1681 108 16
RHODE ISLAND 2461 225 11
SOUTH CAROLINA 1261 235 5
SOUTH DAKOTA 1737 230 8
TENNESSEE 901 171 5
TEXAS 2575 224 12
UTAH 1870 173 11
VERMONT 451 178 3
VIRGINIA 1379 173 8
WASHINGTON 1489 177 8
WEST VIRGINIA 764 132 6
WISCONSIN 2210 131 17
WYOMING 1972 251 8
NATIONAL 1547 188 8

SOUTH DAKOTA 8
KENTUCKY 8
COLORADO 7
MONTANA 7
NORTH CAROLINA 7
FLORIDA 7
LOUISIANA 7
OKLAHOMA 7
MISSOURI 7
NORTH DAKOTA 6
ARKANSAS 6
WEST VIRGINIA 6
ALASKA 6
NEVADA 6
NEW YORK 5
ALABAMA 5
SOUTH CAROLINA 5
TENNESSEE 5
MISSISSIPPI 5
GEORGIA 5
ARIZONA 5
NEW MEXICO 5
IDAHO 4
HAWAII 3
VERMONT 3

Rate per 100,000 residents of each race.
Source: Bureau of Justice Statistics, *Correctional Populations in the United States, 1996,* and Bureau of Census data.

CHAPTER EIGHT
METHODOLOGY

The Methodology used for this research is quantitative in the form of questionnaires and a probability randomization sampling. We will need to look at the popularization of Dayton, Ohio and compare the notion and understanding of law (statues and Constitutional) between African Americans and European Americans. I will use questionnaires to ask 12 questions dealing with simple law and state their nationality, race and age. The questionnaire is designed to display many dynamics of diversity and culture in a particular radius. These dynamics include:

1. Nationality: shows how people classify themselves and the differences that may arise. It can be determined if this is second-class or first-class citizens.
2. Race may reflect the understanding of nationality.
3. Racism is reflected in race, which shows the attitude of the culture.

Questions of the U.S. Constitution, Declaration of Independence and historic court cases (Dred Scott vs. Sanford). The size of the population would be about 100 volunteers. fifty questionnaires would be distributed at a predominantly Black college institution (Wilberforce) and the remaining 50 to a predominantly Black community (Westwood Library). These groups will be classified as Group "A" (Black college) and Group "B" (Black community).

The collection of data acquired through the questionnaire created vital information into the mind of the participant. The objective is find out how much a person knows about the subject. The questionnaire used as a barometer can measure a person's perception of their status. The scores would help the instructor know what a person needs to understand the most. An example of a question would be: *How would you classify yourself? a) African-American B) Black C) American D) African*
Questions tell how a person connects himself or herself to African culture. The limitations to using this form of data will not give an accurate account to a very large populous. It may be like searching for a needle in a haystack. The fact that only 50 questionnaires are given to a group of fairly young (18-25yrs) adults at college will differ from the Black communities, which may offset the accurate percentage of Dayton. Many college students are not from the city of Dayton and may not share the same views. College students were selected because educated energetic people are usually a catalyst for change and progression, which may be a problem with the less educated volunteers at Westwood's Library. Lack of familiarity with politics and current government issues

could create inaccurate responses. Heavily strained incomes play a role on crime and education.

Second objective's limitation is more difficult than primary objective because the delicate subject of religion. Religion has created divisions in the past. Some subject's in both groups have dropped out of class based on their strong belief in a certain religious ideology. The possibility of people not understanding or an unwilling response to new spiritual techniques is high. Many people habitually eat a diet that is contradictory to their historical ancestors. Difficulty in changing a person's diet is high. Diets are usually handed down from one generation to another. Breaking the present cycle of dietary laws is the ultimate goal.

CHAPTER NINE
SUMMARY OF DATA RESULTS

The main goal of this data is to display a lack of information that separates Black citizens in America from their European American counterparts. Chapter five deals with the results from the evaluation plan in chapter 4. Data received from the evaluation plan (questionnaire) will be discussed briefly. Data used from a range of Black college students and urban communities to express the need for Blacks to know history, culture and law.

The objective of citizenship implemented in the data questionnaire with several questions. The purpose for citizenship/nationality questions in the questionnaire display the need to know law. Morality and income played a significant role in a couple of the questions. Morality and income are important to discuss because of the correlation to crime. Many of the questions are simple and designed for 18 years old and up. Majority of these questions were sent by email however, some were physically passed out to a small group. Some participants felt the questions enlightened them or made them aware of what they actually know. It will also prove that Black's need education about the U.S. Constitution and laws passed on their behalf. The questionnaire is a barometer to express a true need to re-educate and show why Black's are second-class citizens in America. Questions asked to a willing participant include: "What are the 13th and 14th Amendments? How do they classify themselves on a job application?" Understanding citizenship means to understand law. Law is the pulse of America's economy and democracy. Citizenship and law intertwine in many questions on the questionnaire. One hundred questionnaires were distributed to a variety of Black people on college campuses and communities. Based on this data, 65% of Blacks in college did not know the 13th Amendment, 50% did not know the 14th Amendment. Seventy percent of Blacks were aware of Dred Scott case however, they did not know exactly the impact of the case. Forty five percent of Blacks consider themselves African American, forty percent Black and fifteen present American. Overall, the questionnaire shows that Blacks are not aware of cultural or legal information. Many consider themselves African American, which is not a lawful citizenship. The survey proves that many do not understand citizenship and nationality. Seventy percent of Black's income on questionnaire was under $50,000. Income has an impact on education, knowledge and morality. Of the 30% with an income over $50,000, 80% of them knew more about the 13th and 14th Amendments, however, nearly 90% still considered themselves African American. Higher incomes may have a positive impact on Black's in criminal incarceration however, traffic stops and racial profiling remains a social problem because of stereotypical mindsets of police based on skin color.

The questionnaire also acts like a preamble to the second objective.

Second objective is re-education of the subject group. The questionnaire prepares group for more instruction. A re-education of subject group is based on History/Nationality and Health/Spiritual. Study classes being held every Monday for 8 weeks. Both subject groups participated in separate study classes dealing with history/nationality and health/spiritual. First four weeks dedicated to History/Nationality and last four weeks on Health/Spiritual. Group "A" classes being held on campus for easy accessibility for college students and group "B" classes at community library. History/nationality familiarized subject groups with intense knowledge of forgotten history and the premise of the Republic of America and the roles Blacks played as Moors in world and American history. Health/Spiritual class informed the groups about better nutrition and history of the "slave" diet with correctional alternatives. Spiritual class deals in esoteric (deep) study on religious text and philosophies to give deeper understanding of the Bible, Koran, Torah and Book of life. Various lectures on DVD and YouTube will be used to give visual and audio understanding.

A test will be giving to both subject groups at the end of 8 weeks. Testing the subject groups on both subjects discussed is the best gauge to seeing results. Testing will be written and actual. Written testing will compose of 20 questions dealing with History/Nationality and Health/Spiritual. An *actual* test is a "hands on" observation of subject groups in real life scenarios. The **actual** test displays the subject's ability to interact in society with results. An example is how to talk to a police officer at a traffic stop. How you let a police officer know your rights as a Moorish American? The tone of voice and response must be acceptable by the instructor. A Mock trial or simulation court trial may be created to test the student's skills in law, orating and attitude. Written questions would include: "What is the Treaty of Peace and friendship of 1787?", "Where does the origin of Moor derive?" and "What does the term *domicile* mean?" Written test is sixty percent of their grade with forty percent for the actual test. Any score under 60% is a failure and student would be instructed to take test over. Passing students from both groups will have the opportunity to proclaim their nationality by filing legal papers stating their nationality and status in America.

The results from our first two groups were somewhat expected. Group A's results were eighty percent passing. Out of the eighty percent passing, nearly sixty percent received an A, eighty percent B and five percent C and seven percent D. When asked, "Did they see a positive change from this course?" seventy percnet said yes. The results were excellent in showing a desire among college students for social change.

Results from Group B were minimal compared Group A. Only fifty-seven passed with firve percent A, ten percent B, and twenty eight percent C and fourteen percent D. Only forty-eight percent felt this course was helpful. The difference was almost a quarter in percentage between the two groups. However the difference, a majority of people passed in both test groups and there was a need to change.

Language usage scores were high. Basic Ki-Swahili is taught in class with little usage outside of curriculum. Simple greetings and questions were taught i.e. Habari Gani (how are you?), Hujambo (hello), Jina lako nani (what's your name?) and Kwa Heri (Goodbye). Group A scored seventy –seven percent passing the Ki-Swahili part of the test. Group B scores sixty five percent passing Ki-Swahili. Group B's scores were slightly lower than Group A's however, participants in the class used the terms outside of class more than college students. Many community volunteers are familiar with Ki-Swahili due to the observance of Kwanzaa.22

---

22 "African-American" holiday created in 1966 by Dr. Maluana Karenga based on Afrikan principles. Kwanzaa uses Ki Swahiilli for its principles. Nguzo Saba are principles which is Swahili for Seven principles. Each principle is Swahili in name. Harambe is Kwanzaa principle which also Swahili for pull together.

CHAPTER TEN
CONCLUSION

The crisis in Black society continues to expand and desolate communities across America. Rampant unemployment, few business resources and limited retail store power increases in urban Black communities. The net worth of an "African American" is still considered under whites and other ethnic groups. Mexican and other "Latino" nationalities are making great strides and in many instances, are passing Blacks with opportunity in America. Slavery is the backdrop for common conditions Blacks continue to face in the 21st century. The psychological and physiological damage of slavery remains to beyond comprehension however, the mental scars are evident. Slavery stripped the African of his culture and nationality, in the effort to subdue and dehumanize. The effects of denationalization created a continuing downward spiral into contemporary times. Lack of nationality separates Black's from all other people on the planet. Denationalization created a second rate citizen that is granted power through privileges and "Civil" rights. First rate Citizens protection comes from human rights and not privileges. Privileges can be taken away by others powerful groups (Congress, legislation).

The primary purpose for this project is education. Re-educating the Black masses about their past identity and lost nationality. Restoration of Black people to first class citizenship is accomplished, through a series of classes and presentations. Classes divided into two primary sections Nationality/History and Health/Spirituality. Under these headings, two subject groups will be analyzed and the data obtained to measure the positive and negative benefits of classes presented. Results and recommendations from these classes will be discussed more in depth later in this chapter.

Understanding of this project has grown tremendously since its beginnings several months ago. Black Nationalism's evolution has emerged in the 21st century, as a necessity for Blacks in America. Analysis of data acquired in the study classes, video lectures, surveys and test results gives hope that Black Nationalism is not dead but a continuing effort to open people to ideals that may have real benefits. The need for Blacks to know law was received well by many subject students. Interest in classes was very important. With 40 students, starting in-group A, 32 remained throughout the entire course. Group B started with 25 students and 15 remained the entire course. Based on the objectives, the project had marginal success.

Objective one dealing with Citizenship was very important to emphasize to the classes. Looking at Group A test results, eighty percent of passed and fifty-seven percent of Group B passed.   The 23-point difference between groups demonstrates a slight breakdown in it appears, based on the statistics that emphasis was actualized.   Findings on the score show that college students would be excellent to introduce Moorish literature. The fact that Black college students in learning institutions receive information effectively.   College students in the past have been the catalyst for grass root movements i.e. SNCC and Civil Rights. Group A's high-test scores were expected in most aspects.   Based on reality, forty percent of Group A's passing class proceeded to become Moorish American Citizens by filing their paperwork to the various agencies. The remaining students who did not continue with Citizenship were interested with possibility of reclaiming Nationality later.   The reality of reclaiming nationality is the challenge directly to the mainstream culture. Changing names from Euro-Centric or made up pseudo urban names into meaningful African names without the restraints of courts or lawyers was some proof that there is validity in the Moorish American phenomenal. Many may be scared that reclaiming nationality may cause problems with social programs i.e. social security, Medicare and taxes. A minority of **Group A** saw it as un-American. Disbelief is reason for skeptics in **Group A**.   The ineffectiveness of reaching the few makes it difficult to unify the group under this objective. I had anticipation that more people would not be receptive to the program. The intervention used with **Group A** made a difference in many ways. Firstly, the knowledge of history gave students of **Group A** confidence with the accomplishment their ancestors, secondly, learning the esoteric meaning of law and its relationship to commerce helped **Group A** understand money and their rights. Learning their rights, **Group A** was able to challenge many codes and ordinances that went unquestioned under normal circumstances. An example of this is with an anonymous student who did not have a driver's license however, because of his new understanding of law. He became a Moorish American after going through class and stopped by police for expired tags and "driving" without a license. Instead of paying the fine, he challenged it in court and not fined. Moorish American class gives students the ammunition to stand up for their Constitutional rights. Overall, I conclude that **Group A** had interest in learning new information.

Group B, as discussed earlier, scores were 20 points lower than **Group A**. Age and environment play key factors in differential statistics among groups. Average age for **Group B** was 35 years old. **Group B** students occupied with work and family, which cuts down on the time they had for other interest. thirty percent of other students were over the age of 50, which often may not pay close attention to details and retain as much information. Older people, in general may want the information for historical reference, however would not see the practicality in being Moorish American. The elderly brought positive feedback to the intervention with wisdom in the form of experience. Comments and stories from the elders make for variables not calculated in the intervention. Despite the lower scores, Group B displayed a promising future. Out of fifty-seven percent of the passing class, only twenty percent became Moorish American. Eighty percent of the new Moorish Americans were men. The women in class seemed more reluctant to join, however they enjoyed the information.

The intervention had limitations that need modification in the future. Intervention for long-term use is realistic and probable. Learning is a lifetime process and takes many years to understand the vast lost knowledge of Moors, their relationship and contributions to the world. Law is complex and cannot be interpreted in a few weeks. Advance (Adept) classes for students looking to get involved in government positions or esoteric knowledge. Study groups remain available to anyone else still seeking African knowledge however not ready to nationalize. The study groups also remain a recruiting ground for people that are more serious.

Policy Recommendation

Based on the data collected, the prescription for this program is to further continuance. The overall performance of the intervention was successful. Students learned and many became Moorish Americans. Recommendations for this program include various suggestions:

1) Change the length of class to 10 weeks. More emphasis directed to the understanding and application of Moorish knowledge. Nationality membership increases with better understanding.
2) Make the class more appealing for woman to equalize the ratio of membership. 3:1 is the present ratio of men to women in nationalization. Include women instructors and feminine attributes of Moorish women.
3) Set more classes in different locations across the city. Using more community libraries and expand the college classes to white universities. Many Black students at white universities go without Afro-centric/Black based groups. Ethno centric ideologies must be balanced among the minorities to create a multi-cultural environment.
4) Expand classes to Black's incarcerated and delinquent juveniles.

5) Moorish/African rights of passage programs, quite possibly already organized, introduced to Moorish youth young adults (community) to counter single parent living.

These recommendations show a need for improvements however, not a deterrent from using the basic principles. The use of this intervention must be continued and expanded to Africans across America. Further research on this topic may include a follow-up report on the students over a period of six months. Monitor the progression of students by having council every three months. Learn if any criminal elements have waned or increased. Ask how they have been able to use their nationality to enhance life. Incorporating partial Moorish knowledge may be useful in religious organizations and Afro-centric groups. Networking with traditional African rights of passage would create Umoja (unity) with pre-existing African/Black organizations. Intervention should include utilizing existing Black/African programs in operation from various social services. The bases of nationality are political, economical and ethnical unity.

Modification is necessary for more inclusive dialogue in spiritual classes. Older and highly religious people considered information offensive in regards to Christianity and Islamic traditions. On the contrary, younger students in **Group A** found spiritual class interesting and refreshing. A level of discernment by the instructor needed to stimulate open minded and religiously committed students.

The nationalization of Black people in America is the focal point to the problems faced in America. Second class citizenship transmitted through Black slave codes, Jim Crow Laws and blatant racism to peoples of African descent for hundreds of years. The results of these acts against humanity have left 299,398,484[23] Blacks disenfranchised with communities' barren of economical resources. This intervention is an opportunity for Blacks to come together based on nationality and become first class Citizens. Like the sovereign "Native Americans" and Catholic Church, MSR OF NK builds on the Sovereignty found by the visionary Noble Drew Ali in 1929.

The process of evolution takes discipline, steadfastness along with guidance. The MSR OF NK is a foundation that builds national, cultural and economical awareness to the Blacks in America. Through educational

---

23 Source U.S. Census Bureau: State and County Quick Facts. Data derived from Population Estimates, Census of Population and Housing, Small Area Income and Poverty Estimates, State and County Housing Unit Estimates, County Business Patterns, Nonemployer Statistics, Economic Census, Survey of Business Owners, Building Permits, Consolidated Federal Funds Report.

programs and collaboration with other African based groups, the MSR OF NK will transform the Black minds and hearts of a second-class people.

APPENDIX: Moorish Science of New Kemit Lesson's in Ki-Swahili/Somo kwanza

Numbers:
Kwanza=First
Moja=one
Mbili=two
Tatu=three
Nne=four
Tano=five
Sita=six
Saba=seven
Nane=eight
Tisa=nine
Kumi=ten

Mimi=I, me
Wewe=you
Yeye=she, he him, her
Sisi=we, us
Ninyi=you pl.
Wao=they, them

Habari=news
Gani=what kind (of)
Habari Zenu?=How are you
-itika=to respond

na=and
la=no
ndiyo=yes
sasa=now
sema=say; kusema=to speak; anasema=s/he is speaking
-fundisha=teach; kufundisha=to teach, teaching
Je=What about?
Anamkiana=to greet
-uliza=ask (a question)
mwingine=another person
Somo=lesson
-toka=come from
unakaa=live
wapa=where
jimbo=state, province
Zeozi=exercise
Nani=who?
Jina=name
Lako=you (as in **your** name)
Lake=his, her

Langu=my, mine
Mzima=health, good condition
Mgeni=guest, stranger
U hali gani=how are you?
i.e. Habari zako; Habari Zano
Jaza=fill in
Namba=number
Ni=is/are
Mwanamume=man
Wanaume=men
Mwanamke=woman
Wanawake=women

1. Jina lako ni nani?=what is your name?

Jina langu ni Bandele=My mane is Bandele
2 Jina lake ni nani?=What is his/her name?
Jina lake ni Tulani.=His name is Tulani
3. Jina langu ni nani?=What is my name?
Jina lako ni Adija=Your name is Adjia

Mimi=me, I
Wewe=you
Yeye=she, he
Sisi=we, us

APPENDIX: THE COLOR LINE

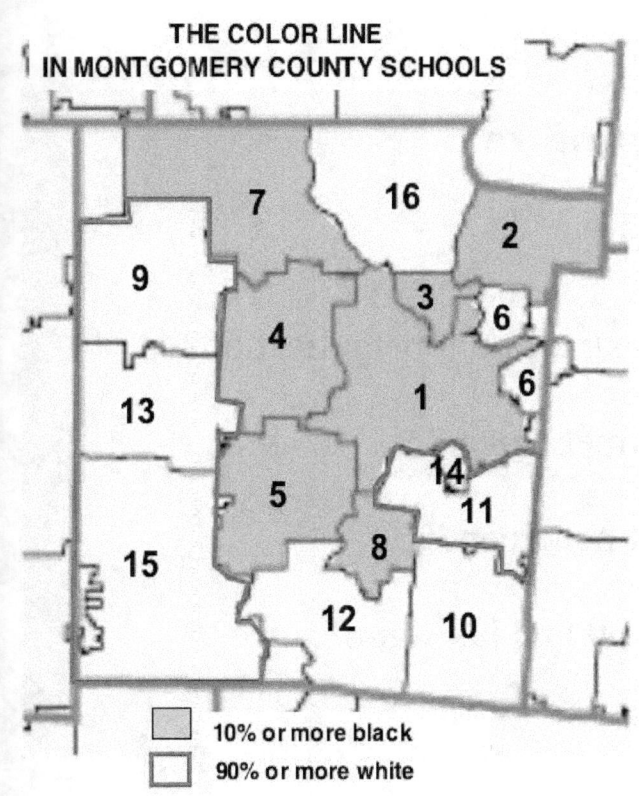

THE COLOR LINE
IN MONTGOMERY COUNTY SCHOOLS

District	%Black	%White
1. Dayton	70.5	23.3
2. Huber Hts	17.5	70.5
3. Northridge	17.0	78.4
4. Trotwood	85.8	9.1
5. Jefferson	78.6	17.6
6. Mad River	8.6	81.9
7. Northmont	15.3	76.4
8. W Carrolton	10.0	81.5
9. Brookville	0.0	98.1
10. Centerville	4.4	84.3
11. Kettering	3.3	91.0
12. Miamisbg	6.1	86.7
13. N Lebanon	0.0	98.3
14. Oakwood	1.0	93.5
15. Valley View	1.0	97.9
16. Vandalia	4.2	89.0

10% or more black
90% or more white

Source:

http://daytonology.blogspot.com/2007_08_01_archive.ht

ml

APPENDIX: QUESTIONAIRE

Questionnaire given to college students and community volunteers pre-class

Survey Questionnaire

1. What is your race?

2. What do you put as race on job application?

3. What is the 13th Amendment?

4. What is the 14th Amendment?

5. Who was Dred Scott and his significance?

6. What is your age?

7. What is your highest-grade level completed in school?

8. What is your nationality?

9. Would you like to visit Afrika? Why?

10. What is your political affiliation?

11. Do you vote?

12. What is your religion?

13. What is Juneteenth?

14. What is your Father's religion? Your mother's religion?

15. Do you celebrate Kwanzaa?

This questionnaire was used by Group A and B prior to any classroom sessions. Questions for readers to answer.

APPENDIX: TRANS-ATLANTIC 1650-1900Trans-Atlantic exports by region

Region	Number of slaves	% accounted for
Senegambia	479,900	4.7
Upper Guinea	411,200	4.0
Windward Coast	183,200	1.8
Gold Coast	1,035,600	10.1
Blight of Benin	2,016,200	19.7
Blight of Biafra	1,463,700	14.3
West Central	4,179,500	40.8
South East	470,900	4.6
Total	10,240,200	100.0

Data derived from tables 1.1, 3.2, 3.4, 4.1 and 7.4 as presented in: *Transformations in Slavery* by Paul E. Lovejoy Cambridge University Press, 2000,

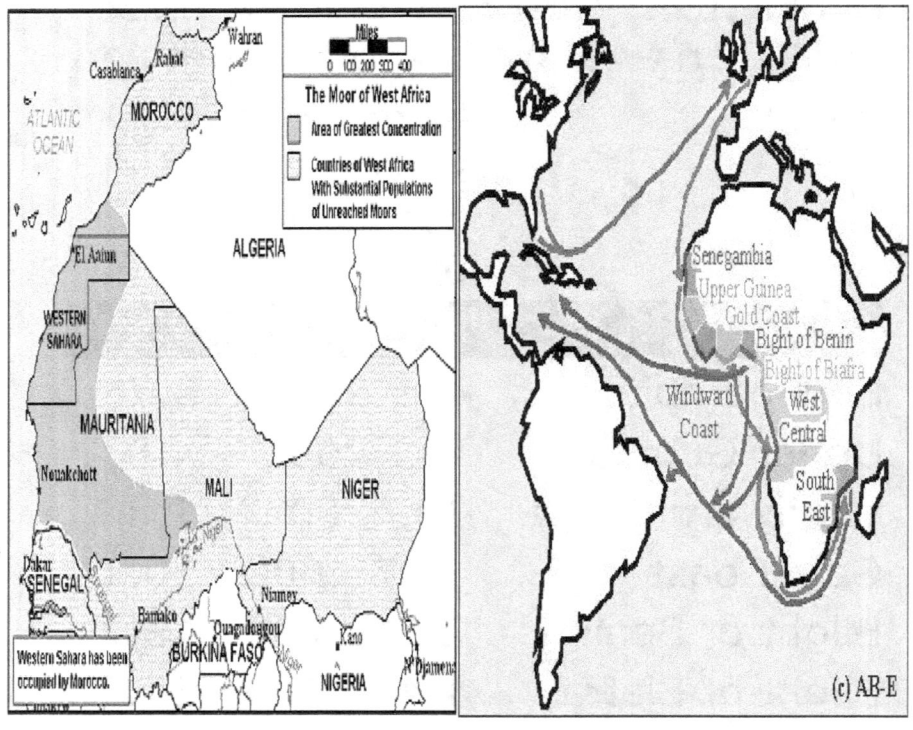

Take a look at the Moors' of West Afrika in comparison to Trans Atlantic slave export region.

Sanhaja[24] is the name of a group of Africans who live on the Saharan fringes of the present day Senegal. They are one of the so-called black people or the sub-Saharan or the tropical Africans. Historically, they are one of the Berber tribes who constituted the main thrust of the Moorish conquest and civilization of Europe.

---

[24] Part of the Great Almoravid dynasty

Reference is made to their phenotype so that it is immediately obvious that we are re-visiting the great history of an unambiguously so-black nation in West Africa. It will be shown here that the place known as West Africa today, is indeed the old heartland of the Moorish Empire which spread on from there to Morocco, Algeria, Tunis, Egypt to Spain, Italy, Palestine, even as far east as India and Indonesia where Moorish descendants still identify themselves by the Moorish designation.[25]

Sylviane A. Diouf, a research scholar at the Schomberg Center for Research on Black Culture and an award-winning author of *Servants of Allah: African Muslims Enslaved in the Americas*, discussed the backgrounds of slaves who were brought to America between 1560 and 1860. At least 100,000 were Muslims, political and religious leaders in their communities, as well as traders, students, Koranic teachers, judges and, in many cases, more educated than their American masters. As slaves, they were prohibited from reading and writing and had no ink or paper. Instead they used wood tablets and organic plant juices or stones to write with. Some wrote, in Arabic, verses of the Koran they knew by heart, so as not to forget how to write. Arabic was also used by slaves to plot revolts in Guyana, Rio de Janeiro and Santo

[25] African Moors: The Sanhajalese Empire – by Jide Uwechia

Domingo because the language was not understood by slave owners. Manuscripts in Arabic of maps and blueprints for revolts were found here as well as in Jamaica and Trinidad.

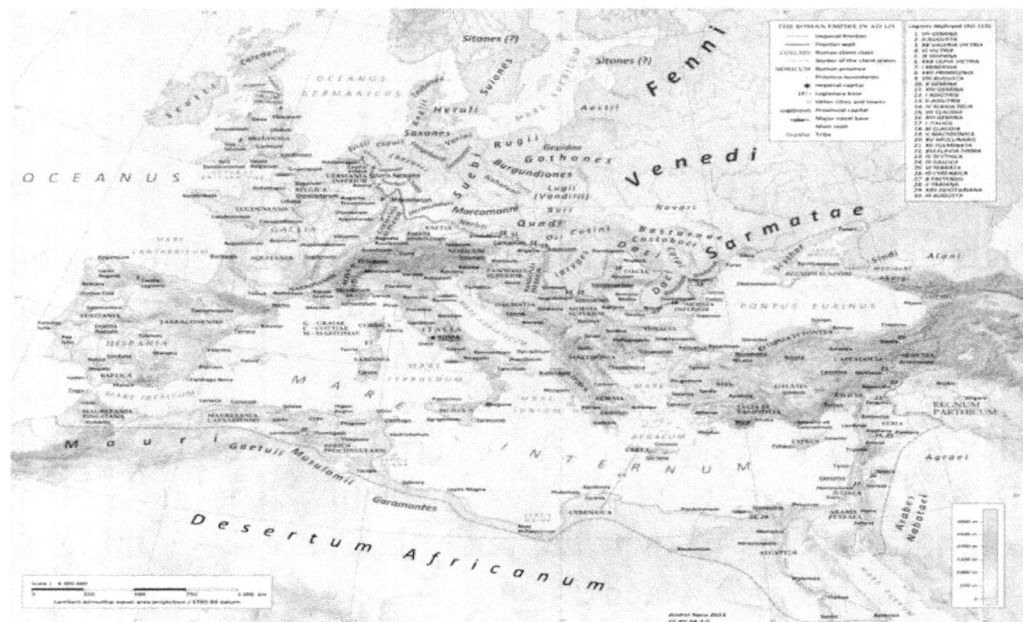

Map of the Roman Empire in 125 a.d. during the reign of emperor **Hadrian. Notice that North Africa is called Mauri.**

With a total population of nearly 3.5 million, the Moors are scattered throughout much of West Africa. Although most of them live in Morocco, Moors can also be found in Mali, Mauritania, Senegal, Niger, and Gambia. They are almost entirely Muslim, as they have been for many centuries. Formerly nomads, large numbers of Moors have settled in urban areas due to recent years of drought. Still, they remain nomadic in spirit.

The Moors have four basic class divisions based on heritage, race, and occupation. The White [Semetic] Moors, making up two-thirds of the group, form the two upper classes; while the Black [African] Moors make up the two lower classes.

APPENDIX: Test Scores for Group A

Grade	% of students
A	60%
B	18%
C	5%
D	7%
F	10%

APPENDIX: Test Score for Group B

A   5%

B   28%

C   14%

D   14%

F   39%

APPENDIX: Test Questions

1. What is your nationality?

2. Habari Gani means what?

3. What is the Treaty of Peace and Friendship w/ Morocco of 1787?

4. What is the definition of a Moor?

5. Who was Noble Drew Ali?

6. Hujambo is the Swahili word for?

7. What is the 13th Amendments?

8. What is the 14th Amendment?

9. Why is the Dred Scott case important?

10. What is the difference between an herb and a drug?

11. What is Common Law?

12. What does the Swahili word *hapana* mean?

13. What is the difference between a *resident* and *domicile*?

14. Should people eat processed foods? Explain?

15. What is a Natural Citizen?

16. What is the Swahili word *ndiyo* mean?

17. What does good-bye in Swahili mean?

18. What is *propia persona* mean?

19. What is Art. 6 Sec. 2 of the U.S. Constitution?

20. What is meditation?

BIBLIOGRAPHY

Ashby, Dr. Muata, *Kemetic Diet: Ancient African Wisdom for Health of Mind, Body and Spirit* Miami, Florida; 2002.

Black's Law Dictionary, 5th ed.,

Black Studies Department, University of Nebraska, Omaha. 1.

Cole David, *No Equal Justice* (The New Press: New York 1999), 142.

The Constitution of the United States with the Declaration of Independence and the Articles of Confederation, Fall River Press, NewYork, NY. 2002. 38.

Diop,Cheikh, Anta, *The Cultural Unity of Negro Africa*, (Presence Africaine, Paris 1963),

Diop, Dr. Cheikh Anta, *TOWARDS THE AFRICAN RENAISSANCE: ESSAYS IN CULTURE AND DEVELOPMENT, 1946-1960.*" Trans. Egbuna P. Modum. London: The Estate of Cheikh Anta Diop and Karnak House, 1996.

Lovejoy,Paul E. *Transformations in Slavery,* Cambridge University Press, 2000

Smallwood,Andrew P. Assistant Professor, *Black Nationalism and the Call for Black Power.*

Willie Lynch Letter and the Making of a Slave. Lushena
   Books 1999, 1

Wilson, Dr. Amos *Blueprint for Black Power*: *A Moral,*
   Political, and Economic Imperative for the Twenty-First
   Century, 27-29.

The World Factbook. Retrieved on 2007-02-22 (Wikipedia)

Living Language *In Flight Swahili Learn Before You Land*, Random House Company.

Other books by Bandele El Amin

Moorish/Muurish Treaties

Wake Up I Free Ka

Holy Koran of Moorish…

Moors, Moabite and Man

Find them on Amazon.com